REWIRE
YOUR
BRAIN

*True changes can occur in
brain for healing*

NASRIN KHAN MD

WRITERS REPUBLIC L.L.C.
515 Summit Ave. Unit R1
Union City, NJ 07087, USA

Website: *www.writersrepublic.com*
Hotline: *1-877-656-6838*
Email: *info@writersrepublic.com*

Ordering Information:
Quantity sales. Special discounts are available on quantity purchases by corporations, associations, and others. For details, contact the publisher at the address above.

Library of Congress Control Number: 2024930173
ISBN-13:   979-8-88536-949-7   [Paperback Edition]
                  979-8-89100-541-9   [Hardback Edition]
                  979-8-88536-950-3   [Digital Edition]

Rev. date: 01/11/2024

Healing is possible by rewriting your brain. Healing is necessary when we are wounded. Wounds can be physical or emotional. A physical wound can be completely healed with the appropriate measures, although a scar may remain. However, to heal emotionally, we have to work long term. In fact, it is an ongoing process.

Sometimes, we might feel like we will never heal. Why is that? Because healing an emotional wound has to happen from within. The healing process has to be initiated inside our brain, and we have to train our brain to stay consistent in all the pathways of brain connections. Our emotional process is connected inside our brain by wiring. Wiring is a neural process. We have different types of emotions, and our brain has different centers for different emotions. We express our emotions by the network of wiring. It's like communicating between different centers, and this network is set in different modes for different emotion. For example, we react differently when we are in pain or when we are in a happy mood. These emotional reactions can also be modified by rewiring.

No one wants to have painful experiences, and for that, we tend to avoid such experiences and suppress those emotions. But by doing this, we are actually not healing. In order to heal, we need to have the mindset of accepting painful experiences, facing challenges, and releasing the negative energy out of our body from the subconscious center, where all the negative energy is stored.

How do you define a trauma?

Trauma is an emotional response to a terrible event, like an accident, rape, or natural disaster. Immediately after the event, shock and denial typically follow. Longer-term reactions include unpredictable emotions, flashbacks, strained relationships, and even physical symptoms, like headaches or nausea.

What is the difference between a wound and trauma?

"Wound" generally refers to skin that has been split, cut, or punctured. "Injury" is a greater term that includes wounds. Thus, a wound is an injury, while vice versa is not correct. For example, a trauma isn't a wound because there is no skin being split, cut, or punctured, but it is an injury since the person getting a trauma has been harmed.

A wound usually refers to physical harm, meaning physical injury, while trauma is emotional harm or injury that might be expressed sometimes through physical symptoms, like headache, nausea, and lightheadedness.

Physical injury is healed through the application of medicine, dressing, and/or ointment. The healing of an emotional trauma occurs differently. The process of healing is initiated and mastered in the brain through neuroplasticity. Neuroplasticity is the process of rewiring.

What is the simple definition of "neuroplasticity"?

Neural plasticity, also known as neuroplasticity or brain plasticity, can be defined as the ability of the nervous system to change its activity in response to intrinsic or extrinsic stimuli by reorganizing its structure, functions, or connections.

It is the ability of the neural network in the brain to change through growth (new growth) and reorganization. It is when the brain functions in a way that differs from the way it usually functions.

The brain is a complex structure, and the emotional brain is even more complex. It consists of the cerebral cortex, the cerebellum, and the brain stem in the middle. The cerebral cortex and the cerebellum are symmetric structures, and the cerebral cortex is responsible for our motor functions. All movements occur and are operated by the cerebral cortex and coordinated by the actions of the cerebellum.

After an injury to the brain by an organic process (for example, a stroke), the brain's neurons are damaged in all aspects, both the motor function and the emotional function, depending on the areas of the brain that are damaged. Motor function recovery is possible by rewiring, by mindfully exercising with the help of rehab therapy. In the same way, emotional trauma can also be healed by rewiring.

In the beginning, it takes focus, effort, and more energy in your brain, but after you make the swing or say hello enough times, it becomes effortless. It's just like any exercise. As you practice more and more, it becomes a habit. Thus, to rewire your brain, you will have to maintain the new behavior long enough to make it become fairly automatic. In time, practice will make it effortless.

Through neuroplasticity, anyone can rewire or reorganize the brain to make it function to achieve the desired outcome. Plasticity means malleability, moldability. You can literally rearrange networking to make connections among the different areas of your brain and retrain your emotional brain to activate your desired feeling level.

Rewiring is necessary when you suffer from trauma caused by negative energies traveling within your brain centers. These negative energies originate from core feelings that were blocked and accumulated in the subconscious center. If these negative energies are never released, they will be trapped in the subconscious center.

Human beings are susceptible to pain, and as humans don't want to suffer from pain, they tend to avoid these painful experiences instead of facing and dealing with them. That's when these negative energies are trapped, building tremendous negative energies inside the mind and body, and the person can never heal.

Why is neuroplasticity important?

We can influence our brain development in positive or negative directions. We can exercise on focusing more on positivity and consistently and consciously change the outcome. Achieving the expected outcome is a positive experience, and we can do that by neuroplasticity, meaning rearranging the network. So how do we change the network? This can be done by repetitive stimulation using a painful stimuli. It's ironic, right? But the mechanism is exactly like the acupuncture mechanism.

In rehab medicine, chronic pain is treated by acupuncture. What is acupuncture? To describe acupuncture, I have to describe the physiology of pain pathway. The pain pathway has sensory nerve endings, which carry painful signals after getting stimulated by the afferent nerve, through interneurons in the cell body, and to the brain. The brain senses this painful stimuli, and this stimuli travels through the efferent nerve back to the nerve ending at the site of the stimuli. That's when the body site feels the pain.

Acupuncture treats this pain by repeatedly sending the pain stimuli to ultimately desensitize the area so that you won't feel pain anymore, meaning the source of pain is still there but you don't feel pain. Through neuroplasticity, you can do the same exercise to treat emotional pain. That's when healing occurs.

So what you do is bring up painful memories repeatedly. Initially, you will feel more pain, but eventually, you will heal. The more we engage and challenge our mind and body, the longer our brain will function at a higher level. There are also many other benefits to encouraging neuroplastic change.

How does it work?

A neuroplastic change occurs at the chemical, structural, and functional levels of the brain. These changes work in concert with one another.

A chemical change occurs in the initial stages of learning something new. It primarily influences short-term memory or short-term improvement in a motor skill.

A structural change occurs when neurons in the brain change their connections, altering your brain structure. This type of change requires more effort and time. It involves long-term memory and long-term improvement of a motor skill.

A functional change occurs when all of the brain's networks change. These brain networks, as they are used over and over again, become more excitable and more efficient when activated.

Neuroplastic exercise

Begin by selecting an activity that is new, challenging, and important to you. Commit yourself to engaging in the exercise as frequently as you can. You will further your neuroplastic change if you also eat a healthy diet, exercise regularly, and connect with others. You can also do the following:

- Learn a new language.
- Learn to play an instrument.
- Visit a different part of the city, state, or country.
- Go to a museum or concert.
- Cook new food items or listen to a different type of music.
- Practice mindfulness.
- Experiment with three good things.
- Try brain aerobics.
- Use your alternate hand to brush your teeth or write.
- Get dressed while keeping your eyes closed.
- Buy groceries at a different store.

What is self-directed neuroplasticity?

You can rewire your brain consciously through self-directed neuroplasticity. It is the ability to create new neural connections inside your brain, and how do you do that? By mindful practice. Mindfulness and Meditation.

Mental Training of Mindfulness meditation is no different than other forms of skill acquisition that can induce Neuroplasticity.

Mindfulness exercise strengthen the neural circuit involved in voluntary control of attention through repeated practice in focusing attention. Consistent mindfulness practice can change the way you think, act and feel because it can literally change your brain.

Self-directed neuroplasticity is when you intentionally rewire your brain to create positive habits.

What is habit?

Humans do things in their subconscious mind—automatically. Yes, the term is a mindful, but it's also a powerful, science-based method to break undesirable habits and create new, healthy ones.

The concept was first defined by researcher Dr. Jeffrey Schwartz and then popularized by Dr. Rick Hanson, a psychologist and senior fellow at UC Berkeley's Greater Good Science Center and author of *Hardwiring Happiness*.

Self-directed neuroplasticity is different from experience-dependent neuroplasticity, a passive process in which we reinforce habits by doing them unconsciously over and over again, whether they're good or bad.

You can use this method to train your brain to stick with habits for the long haul. Does it sound too good to be true? Read on to learn how to do it.

A neuroplasticity primer

- Neuroplasticity is the brain's ability to change throughout your life.
- Experience-dependent neuroplasticity is the passive process of reinforcing habits by doing them unconsciously over and over again, whether they're good or bad.
- Self-directed neuroplasticity is the active process of consciously reflecting on how habits make us feel.

How habits are formed

A habit is a routine or ritual has become almost automatic or second nature. It is an activity you repeat so regularly that it can be hard to change. This can be biting your nails when you're worried, picking up a bottle of wine whenever you pass the liquor store, or cracking open a bag of chips while watching TV at the end of the day.

A habit may also be something you do unconsciously, like jiggling your leg while you're on a flight or licking your lips when you're forced to do some public speaking.

But where do habits come from?

Your sensory nervous system is always monitoring for actions you can take that will deliver a hit of dopamine, the brain's reward chemical. We're wired to seek out pleasure.

"Any habit we develop is because our brain is designed to pick up on things that reward us and punish us," explains Dr. Sanam Hafeez, a clinical psychologist and neuropsychologist based in New York City.

When your brain recognizes a pattern, such as a connection between action and satisfaction, it files that information away neatly in an area of the brain called the basal ganglia. This is also where we develop emotions and memories, but it's not where conscious decisions are made—that's the prefrontal cortex.

This may be what makes habits so hard to break. They come from a region of the brain that's out of your conscious control, so you're barely aware you're doing them, if at all. That means habits are subconscious, and if it is a good habit, it does not affect your mental health, and there's no negative impact on your emotional health. So anyone can have a happy subconscious mind.

But when bad habits occur subconsciously, they negatively affect your health, both physical and mental health. In fact, physical health and mental health are linked to each other.

Let me describe the effect of dopamine on your emotional health. Dopamine is a happy chemical neurotransmitter. The more dopamine released in your body, the happier you are.

That's why nowadays everyone talks about thinking positively and verbalizing affirmations, literally saying positive words out loud. These will actually release dopamine, and you will feel happy. By constantly verbalizing positive words, you are actually rewiring your brain. That means a new neural connection is happening inside your brain.

In the early days of humankind, this was beneficial. The reward center of our brains was a survival tool that helped us seek out the things we needed to survive (like comfort and calories) and avoid discomfort. In a modern world, though, that constant search for feel-good experiences can drive us into some less-than-helpful directions.

Just because something feels good in the moment, that doesn't mean it's good for our long-term happiness, health, longevity, social relationships, or mental wellness. And just because something is uncomfortable, that doesn't mean it's dangerous.

Just like in our ancestors, our brains chase that dopamine high. So when a behavior comes along that results in a reward, the brain builds a connection between that behavior and pleasure that can be hard to shake.

This link of cue, action, and reward is how a habit is born.

So how long does the process of rewiring your brain take? Well, the short answer is, it depends.

It's been popularly suggested that it takes 10, 000 hours to be skillful at something. Other research suggests that it takes up to 10 weeks to develop a new habit. In reality, however, the time it takes to develop a new skill or different behavior depends largely on the individual and on other personal factors.

You can speed up the formation of new neural pathways in your brain by working with your subconscious mind.

Now that you know how neuroplasticity works, you know that to rewire your brain, your neurons need to be stimulated via repetition and activity. Generally, this is a slow process, but it can be accelerated by reprogramming your mind.

How does reprogramming your mind help increase neuroplasticity?

Let's say you want to rewire your brain to make yourself an artist. Changing your brain's internal wiring will require you to mimic the thought and habit patterns of a painter or any other artist you want to become until it becomes second nature to you.

The problem arises when you aren't consistent.

If you want to be healthy, think about this. Say, after coming home from the gym, your subconscious decides to reward your workout with a treat—for example, your favorite ice cream. In your subconscious, this is neither good nor bad. It is simply trying to ease your pain with pleasure.

By reprogramming your mind, however, you can tell to your subconscious that working out is an act of self-love. You love yourself, so this, therefore, is a pleasure and a reward. Eating ice cream, on the other hand, is harmful and counterproductive. After you consistently rewire your brain or reprogram, you may discover that you enjoy working out more. You may also notice that you enjoy eating ice cream less (or even not at all).

Once you reprogram your mind, it becomes a lot easier for you to stay consistent with your health and fitness goals. With discipline and practice, the synapses that encourage positive behavior become stronger, and exercising and eating healthy food almost immediately becomes second nature for you.

The same technique works on every aspect of your life. You rewire your brain when you need to heal, right? So your work of rewiring or reprogramming is necessary only if you have too many negativity inside your subconscious. And trust the process that if you are consistent on exercising rewiring process, healing is possible.

Let me describe the healing process. There are six steps.

The first step is deep relaxation. This is usually done by being in a comfortable position, like sitting or lying down (it can be any position), and focusing on your breathing.

The second step is awareness. Be aware of what is happening. What is your emotional state at the moment, and what is it bringing into your consciousness? All the negativity or negative energies are trapped in the subconscious, and to release these energies, you have to be aware of these negative energies because these are in your subconscious. So being aware means being conscious.

The third step is accepting. Accepting your situation or your negative circumstances is the key to happiness. Most of the time, we humans try to change what is outside of us. We try to resist our circumstances when the situation is outside of our expectation, but we do not realize that it is not within our control. To change someone or anything beyond our own control is impossible unless someone is motivated to change the circumstances for a positive outcome.

For example, in a relationship between two persons, both have their own feelings and emotions. You don't know what is going on in their emotional brain, so to change them, they will have to work on their emotions and feelings. It's the same for our own healing. We will have to work within ourselves.

Accepting the situation is a step to take for healing. Healing is necessary when you have painful experiences. We usually try to avoid painful experiences and want to do something so that we don't need to deal with pain, but that's rejecting, not accepting. To heal, we have to accept painful experiences.

The fourth step is witnessing—witnessing what happens when you experience negative painful situations. What are your emotions and feelings? There are differences between feelings and emotions.

Feeling is your core feeling after going through a negative experience—for example, feeling sad, happy, not heard or loved, rejection, not worthy of being loved, neglected. Emotion is when energies from the core feeling are blocked. They get trapped in the subconscious center, like depression, anxiety, angry, resentment. When you react to your emotional struggles, all negative experiences occur.

The fifth step is direct experience. When a real situation occurs, you are in fight mode, but when you are trying to process your negative energy to heal you, try to imagine those negative circumstances and experience the pain directly. It is hard because no one wants to experience pain, but in order to heal, you have to process the negative energy and release it. Unless you release your negative energy trapped in your subconscious, you cannot heal.

The sixth step is releasing, which means letting go of all the negativities.

Rearranging your brain is possible by doing the above steps consistently.

After about ten weeks, as discussed above, you will be able to feel the change. You will have soul peace. Circumstances that used to bother you will not give you pain anymore.

When I was a child, I used to cry on every little instances of discomfort. Why? It's because I didn't have the maturity about how to first identify my feelings and emotions. Also, I didn't know how to process and release. Slowly, as I go through experiences, mostly painful experiences produce negative energies, and as we don't know how to process and release, these energies get trapped and build up in our subconscious. When we continue to reject negative, painful experiences because we don't want to suffer from pain, more negative energies accumulate in the subconscious.

It is well known in psychology that when you have a pool of negative energies in your subconscious, you actually attract more negative experiences or circumstances in your life. That happens without your consciousness. You don't even realize that you are attracting negative circumstances. For example, if you are traumatized in your early childhood, if you were neglected and abused, if your voice was never heard, your subconscious is all full of core feelings: anger, frustrations, resentful. You will always feel in your subconscious mind that you are not good enough, that you are not worthy enough to be heard or respected.

In fact, you will subconsciously attract more people around you who will always try to suppress you, disrespect you, ignore you, bully you, or will make fun of you. In fact, even when choosing a life partner, unconsciously, you will be with the person who has a narcissistic trait meaning will always suppress you and will make you the bad person in front of the whole world.

So it is very important to consciously work on yourself to heal. The work is rewiring your brain.

When I mentioned the third step, acceptance, I meant accepting the feelings and emotions in your subconscious due to the circumstances. These circumstances could be normal or positive experiences, but your perception could be different due to your past experiences that produced negative energies. Then you start to reject and avoid painful experiences because you think that by rejecting or not accepting this painful experience, you will not feel pain.

But actually by doing this process, you are creating more negative energies trapped in your subconscious. Unless you process negative energies and release them to clear the trapped energies, you will never heal. Accepting the feeling and actually experiencing pain will ultimately help you heal. Accepting does not mean you have to accept new painful experiences. You have to release your subconscious first. Then only you can avoid attracting negative experiences. It takes time, but it is possible.

I am 55 years old, and I am still working on myself to clear my subconscious.

Being the youngest among five siblings, I was never taken seriously, and my opinion didn't matter to any of my siblings. Whatever I say, they laugh and then start to talk about me as if I know nothing. I was as smart as my other siblings; in fact, I was smarter than some of them. But I was never acknowledged, so I started to build negative energies in my subconscious. So the wiring of my brain network was set as "No connection is working."

I was not good enough. I was not worthy. My other siblings were better than me. Throughout my life, I was rejecting my feelings, and to avoid those experiences of bullying and disrespect, I would try to compensate by doing more for them. I always went out of my way to please them occasionally, and the cost was physical tiredness. But did it help me? No. Instead, they started to use me more because I gave them power over me instead of working on myself.

Very recently, I've started to work on rewiring my brain, and it works like miracle. I don't let them control me anymore. I consciously and constantly rewire my brain. I am mindful about the negative feeling, and as soon as I identify negative energy, I process those by relaxing, identifying, accepting, witnessing, directly experiencing, and finally, releasing.

Releasing means letting go of the feeling, not reacting. Even if I react, I react with a calm brain so that I don't lose my control. Once you hit the threshold of tolerance, the fight-and-flight response starts, which is an automatic physiological reaction to an event that is perceived as stressful or frightening. The perception of this threat activates the body to either fight or flee.

The fight-or-flight response is characterized by increased heart rate, anxiety, increased perspiration, tremors, and increased blood glucose level. All these are harmful to the heart, and because this is an automatic reaction, unless you are consciously working on your stress level, experiencing these symptoms are inevitable. And that's the reason you have to start working on your stress level and making sure it doesn't cross the threshold.

When the fight-and-flight response is triggered, there is also an increase in the release of hormones like epinephrine from the adrenal gland. Epinephrine increases heart rate and force of contraction, increasing the output, eventually raising blood pressure. This way, you get physically sick.

That's why rewiring is very important for your well-being. The rewiring process should be started as soon as you can sense that stressful situations may come.

Usually, we tend to avoid or reject painful situations because we don't want to suffer from pain. We think avoiding the incoming stressful situations is the way to heal, but this is a misconception. By avoiding these situations, we are actually accumulating more negativity in our subconscious, which will attract more negative circumstances. We don't realize this because it happens subconsciously. That's why the rewiring process involves being aware of painful situations and processing these negative energies, meaning you are constantly rewiring your brain.

One of the ways to release negative energy is writing down your negative experiences in a piece of paper, imagining those experiences (even actually speaking out loud about those experiences), and saying to yourself, "I accept myself as I am. I love myself. I am not at fault for the circumstances, and I was hurt by someone significant. Now I want to release myself from these painful experiences." You can write down all your negative experiences and imagine that those experiences are happening now. You feel the pain, but you don't act out. And then just let go of the feeling. If you practice this every day, eventually, you will be able to have no negative feelings at all because by that time, you will have rewired your brain.

"I did my best today." So what does saying this mean? You can always practice saying this sentence: "I did my best today." The thing is the purpose. My interpretation of this sentence is this: If your day goes according to however you want it to go, then of course, you will be happy. You'll think "My entire day today was the best day!" because you've done your best. But if the day does not go according to however way you want it, you need to rewire your brain. You can say, "I did my best. Even though the day became worse, still, I did my best."

That is one way of rewiring or rebuilding your brain connection. By practicing this, one day, you will realize that your brain has been rewired in a peaceful state. It means, within your brain, the process of neuroplasticity has occurred. This is where neuroplasticity is important. Neuroplasticity means rewiring your brain.

Why do you rewire your brain? It's for healing, right? Or for a healthy lifestyle. Let me describe this healing.

What is neuroplasticity healing?

Neuroplasticity healing refers to the lifestyle changes and brain exercises that can help the neural connections in your brain continue developing and changing.

For physical healing, you need medications along with physical exercise, a healthy diet, and lifestyle changes. We hear this often in medical practice, right? Why do all clinicians stress on these? It's because, by changing your lifestyle (which involves a healthy diet and physical exercise), you are going toward your goal, which is to remain healthy. Right? But if your emotional health is not stable, your physical health will not be stable as well. This means that no matter how much physical exercise you do, if you don't combine physical exercise with brain exercise, your overall healing (physical and mental) will not occur.

Some diet and lifestyle changes can help increase neuroplasticity, along with overall health. There are also a number of programs aimed specifically at retraining the brain and the nervous system and reprogramming emotional responses. These may be referred to as neuroplasticity training, limbic system retraining, or amygdala retraining.

Neuroplasticity healing programs typically involve a combination of meditation, breath work, visualization, and behavioral exercises.

What is the limbic system?

To understand the neuroplasticity training or healing, I will have to describe the limbic system.

The limbic system is composed of structures in the brain that are involved in regulating one's behavior, emotion, and memory. These include the thalamus, basal ganglia, pineal gland, hippocampus, cerebrum, cerebellum, hypothalamus, pituitary gland, and amygdala.

The amygdala is one component of the limbic system and is connected to emotional memory and response, including the fight-or-flight response to danger or stress. The amygdala plays a major role in emotional reaction, so amygdala retraining or rewiring is very, very important in the healing process.

Limbic system retraining is the basis of healing from trauma.

The benefits of neuroplasticity healing or limbic system retraining

Although research into this topic is still in its primitive state, some studies suggest that limbic system retraining programs may lead to the following benefits:

- Pain reduction for those with fibromyalgia or chronic fatigue syndrome
- Reduced anxiety
- Improved stress response
- Increased mindfulness (main brain rewiring process)
- Better sleep
- Increased energy
- Reduced levels of depression

One 2020 pilot randomized controlled trial involving patients with fibromyalgia found that, compared to a relaxation therapy, an amygdala retraining program led to improvements in pain, anxiety, and depression, as well as mindfulness and self-compassion [1].

What's really interesting about this study is that three months after treatment had ended, the limbic system retraining group was still experiencing not only improved pain and symptoms but significant improvements in pain catastrophizing and psychological rigidity. In other words, it wasn't just their pain that had improved, but their *response* to pain, as well as their mental or emotional ability to cope.

The fact that our brains can create and strengthen neural pathways when we learn or are faced with something new is a good thing.

According to the limbic system or amygdala theory, the nervous system may have learned to become overly sensitive or responsive to certain triggers, even after they've stopped being harmful.

For example, you might have painful experiences after you were rejected by your boyfriend or husband, you were not loved the way you want to be loved, you were suppressed by your parents or your older siblings, or you felt rejected. So your core feeling is rejection, and your secondary feeling is sadness, anger, or resentfulness. In this case, your brain has learned to be overly sensitive to these painful stimuli. So later on, even if are just witnessing any of these circumstances happening to others, not even to you, it might trigger your brain neurons to overly react, and you also experience emotional pain, even though there is no direct stimuli to you. This is because you have not healed in the first place. This is subconscious.

Here's another example: If you have dealt with reactivity to food or supplements for several months or even years, paired with chronic symptoms (like fatigue, brain fog, bloating, or constipation), your limbic system may have learned to associate food, supplements, or mild symptoms with danger. Even if you've healed your gut, improved the health of your immune system, and resolved the majority of the underlying issues that led to your symptoms, your brain can still respond to food or any hint of symptoms the way it's been trained to—essentially, by making you anxious.

And that's where neuroplasticity healing or training comes in. The goal is to rewire those neural pathways and reprogram these responses that may be keeping you in a state of trauma or pain even after your body has healed and, in the case of emotional trauma, even when you don't have ongoing painful experiences.

A healthy gut is linked to a healthy brain

A healthy gut is a neuroplasticity booster. This means that by following a specific diet, you can maintain your gut health secondarily, improving brain health.

This is how you can do that:

- Reducing brain inflammation through
  o An anti-inflammatory diet
  o Improving the health of your gut bacteria
- Getting better sleep (or improving your sleep hygiene)
- Physical activity

Let's go through some of these areas in more detail.

Neuroplasticity, cognition, and your gut

A sluggish brain and poor cognitive function may actually relate to what is going on with your gut bacteria. The science linking the brain and gut health is far from fully developed, but it shows the following:

- There is a constant two-way communication from your microbiota to your brain and the other way around via the nervous and immune systems and hormonal signaling.
- Disruptions to your microbiome can impair these communication pathways between the gut and the brain.
- The microbiome also influences gut production of important transmitters (such as dopamine, serotonin, and GABA), which play a key role in affecting mood.

Brain inflammation is one of the primary contributory factors to brain fog and may also reduce neuroplasticity. Unfortunately, imbalances in the gut microbiome have been shown to produce inflammation in the brain.

Cognitive symptoms, like brain fog, have also been associated with irritable bowel syndrome (IBS), Crohn's disease, small intestinal bacterial overgrowth (SIBO), and gluten sensitivity, further reinforcing a gut–brain link.

Brain boost diet

Avoiding food that cause inflammation (such as sugar, alcohol, deep-fried food, and highly processed foods) is your first step toward healthier brain function. To have a healthy brain (meaning a neuroplastic brain), the first step is to have a healthy diet.

So what does a healthy diet entail? Most healthy diets include plenty of anti-inflammatory food, which encourages a more neuroplastic brain. These are unprocessed food, polyphenols, found in colorful vegetables and fruits, tea, and some herbs. Eating these are linked with improved neuroplasticity, which helps in rewiring the brain.

"Eating whole" while cutting out the junk is a way of eating healthy.

I understand that processed food is tasty, and we do have a tendency to eat more processed food and junk food, especially when we are stressed. But it is ironic that we think in our mind that eating junk food will make us feel better. It is like being addicted to alcohol and drugs. People tend to relieve their stress by drinking or doing drugs, but does it solve the problem? No, right? It actually increase problems more by making you physically ill due to alcohol and drug-related physical sickness.

So mindful practice or rewiring your brain to healthy habits (e.g., eating a healthy diet) is one part of neuroplasticity exercise.

Be mindful about these diets. See the food items below:

The Mediterranean diet, which is rich in polyphenols, has been the most tested for its impacts on cognitive function. For example:

- A 2016 review of thirty-two studies associated the Mediterranean diet with improved cognitive function, a decreased risk of cognitive impairment, and decreased risk of dementia. However, results were not consistent and some of the studies reviewed found no association between diet and improved cognitive function.
- A 2018 systematic review found that a Mediterranean diet improved 12.1% of outcomes on cognitive tests. Overall, the researchers found that the evidence was inconclusive but noted the significant cognitive improvements.

There are also good reports of cognitive improvements from patients who are following a Paleo diet. The Paleo and Mediterranean diets are very similar, but the Paleo diet also cuts down on carbs. It also restricts gluten and dairy, which are some of the most common food intolerances.

Whichever diet you choose, aim to include plenty of oily fish as its omega-3 content has been linked with better cognition. There is an unproven belief that Asian people have sharp memory and that it is linked to eating fish. It makes sense, right? Oily fish has increased amounts of omega-3 fatty acid, which improves cognition.

So add to your main meal fish like salmon, sardines, etc.

Quality sleep

Most people need seven to eight hours of good-quality sleep a night to ensure good cognitive function and maintain good neuroplasticity. Neurology research shows us that a good night's sleep improves learning outcomes, restores the synapses (junctions) between nerve cells (neuroplasticity, new neurons, and synapses), solidifies memories, and removes brain waste. These are all examples of rewiring or neuroplasticity. On the other hand, lack of sleep can lead to a leaky gut, which can contribute to systemic inflammation, including brain inflammation.

Monitoring your sleep is worth investing in. Do you know what sleep hygiene is? Having routine in your daily life is very important. Sleep hygiene is discipline. Set a specific time for your sleep, make your bedroom only for sleep (meaning don't keep a TV or any other devices in the bedroom). Turn off your cell phone, laptop, or any other devices at least thirty minutes before your bedtime. If possible, try not to have any negative thoughts during your bedtime. Try to recite positive affirmations, and you will find see slowly falling asleep. Then you will have a peaceful sleep and will not have vivid dreams. And you will wake up fresh and energetic with good energy and positive energy. Positive energy means your brain network is well formed and well connected to each part in the limbic system, which is an important part of your emotional health.

Be mindful of maintaining good sleep hygiene.

Regular exercise

Daily exercise is vital for concentration, focus, and mood. Each week, you should try to fit in 150 minutes of moderate exercise or 75 minutes of vigorous exercise. This can be spread over several short bursts (5–10 minutes) if you prefer.

Research shows that working out provides the following benefits [30]:

- Improvement of neuroplasticity by altering the structure and function of synapses in parts of the brain (including the hippocampus, which plays a big role in learning and memory)
- Increase of the density and size of cortical neurons (nerve cells in the brain's cortex), which can also positively impact memory, attention, and perception

When you raise your heart rate and work up a sweat, levels of brain-derived neurotrophic factor (BDNF) also rise. BDNF is a molecule with a key role in neuroplastic changes related to beneficial learning and memory [31].

More generally, exercise helps to decrease systemic inflammation and improve sleep quality—two factors that can directly affect cognitive function [32, 33].

In older people, research shows that exercise may improve mild cognitive impairment [34].

Probiotics for the gut–brain axis

When you've already taken steps to eat well, sleep better, and get moving, you can support these new foundations with probiotic supplements, which feed your gut with healthy bacteria.

The idea that probiotics can be very helpful in promoting mental health and wellness is more than just theoretical. Scientific research shows that probiotics can provide the following benefits:

- Prevent inflammatory neurodegeneration
- Improve cognition in patients with IBS, fibromyalgia, and Alzheimer's
- Improve moods in people with mild to moderate depression, potentially alleviate major depressive disorder, and have an anti-anxiety effect

- Relieve stress and enhance memory, social emotional cognition, and verbal learning for adults who have been experiencing emotional stress

Other neuroplasticity healing tips and tricks

Some evidence suggests that you may also get cognitive gains through certain kinds of supplements, brain training games, and even sauna therapy.

Supplements for cognitive enhancement

If your diet and lifestyle foundations are in place and your cognition needs some fine-tuning, supplements may be of help. A few research-backed options for improving cognitive function include lion's mane, citicoline ashwagandha, ginkgo biloba, and turmeric. Turmeric is now the top story because of its antioxidant effect. Indians and Bangladeshis eat a lot of turmeric. Their main dishes are rice with curry, and in curries, they use a lot of turmeric.

Brain training

The theory behind brain training aids and apps is that they use techniques from the world of neuroscience to offer targeted mental stimulation. In turn, this reorganizes connections between brain cells, improving brain neuroplasticity.

- One study found that young adults who used brain training games had gains in brain processing speed, working memory, and executive functions, like flexible thinning and self-control.
- A 2020 systematic review and meta-analysis involving adults over sixty years old without cognitive impairment found that computerized brain training programs also significantly improved their processing speed, working memory, executive function, and verbal memory, but not their attention or visual-spatial processing.

Sauna therapy

If you have access to a sauna, this could be another way to give yourself a brain boost. The evidence here isn't strong, but it's intriguing. For example, observational studies have the following results:

- Young men's brains are more relaxed and more efficient at performing auditory and visual tasks 90 minutes after sauna bathing.
- People who took saunas 9–12 times a month are less likely to develop dementia than those who took saunas 0–3 times a month.

Exactly why saunas are so beneficial is uncertain. However, heat therapy can cause the activation of heat shock proteins, which may be part of the brain's way of healing itself from neurodegenerative attacks. It also benefits muscle function and brain blood flow.

In addition to the potential mental health benefits, saunas (and other heat and soak therapies) have been shown to have physical benefits, including the following:

- Improving cardiovascular health and reducing high blood pressure
- Reducing stress and chronic pain
- Improving metabolism markers, like fasting blood glucose

More research is needed, but if you have the opportunity to take a hot bath or sauna on a regular basis, it's worth doing. After all, it's a very soothing thing to do anyway. And it is recreational therapy. There is no way you will not feel better or relaxed after a sauna bath.

The bottom line

In summary, you can encourage an adaptable, neuroplastic, healthy brain by working on your diet, sleep, and exercise. And if you feel like you've hit a wall with your treatment for chronic illness or symptoms, a neuroplasticity or limbic system retraining program may be able to help.

Sometimes, unpacking what aspect of your diet or lifestyle may be causing your brain fog or lack of focus is hard to do without professional help. Consider making an appointment with a therapist (psychologist and/or life coach) who can assist you in this neuroplasticity training and help you rewire your brain for an effective and permanent result.

Eating a healthy diet, exercising, sleeping—these are all necessary to stay healthy physically. This is what we think, but these are all tips for maintaining your mental stability too.

When we face stressful situations, there is increased release of cortisol levels inside our body. Cortisol is called the stress hormone. This in turn raises your heart rate, blood pressure, and blood sugar. And we all know how these can affect our physical health along with our mental health. Mental health and physical health are closely linked.

Cutting off negative people from our life is also a part of rewiring our brain. How is that possible? You might be questioning this concept.

Imagine negative people as painful stimuli inside your body. When painful stimuli are in your peripheral nerves, these are then carried to your brain, which is central to your body. The brain perceives these stimuli as painful stimuli and send the signal back to your periphery.

Thus, you feel pain. Negative people cause trauma to you and give you pain this way.

Now to get relief from pain, what do we do? We either remove the painful stimuli if we can or we take medicine, which removes pain by blocking the whole network or pathway. By doing this, we are rewiring our brain. So if we can remove the negative and toxic people from our life, we are actually rewiring our brain. Eventually, we can heal this way.

However, completely removing all negative people is not always possible. Even after cutting off those people, we still have aftereffects. I am comparing these aftereffects with toxic memories. We have memories in the brain that are actually in our subconscious (what I described earlier), and that's why we need to exercise retraining our brain on processing these negative energies and releasing it for a complete healing.

In the whole world, there are negative or toxic people everywhere, so cutting off negative people from your life will make you feel very lonely. So initially, practicing neuroplasticity and cutting off negative people might be very challenging for us, and we may feel like we will never heal or will be able to rewire our brain.

But let me give you my own example. I faced many problems dealing with negative people in my life, and these are people whom I used to think as my friends. I started to explore, and my passion started to grow. I fulfilled my dream by doing some challenging activities to help the community. I started to realize that all these people whom I used to consider as my friends were actually not my true friends. They were toxic and negative people and never considered me as their friend because if they did, they would have supported me in my activities.

Instead, they became my enemies. Out of insecurity and jealousy, they started to isolate me from their group. I felt lonely, and these microtraumas were constantly giving me pain. But by practicing meditation and mindfulness and by staying strong and firm, I realized that I did not need those negative people in my life. As soon as I cut them off, I felt at peace. In fact, I am still struggling with these people and I am still affected by memories of them. I thought they were lovely memories, but in fact, they were aftereffects, meaning they were negative experiences stored in my subconscious.

I am trying to process these negative energies and release them permanently, and when I'm able to process some negative energies and release them, I feel peaceful. The circumstances that give me pain do not happen anymore because I don't allow them to break my boundaries.

To heal and rewire our brain, we have to set up boundaries.

By setting up boundaries, we are keeping our inside environment peaceful, positive, and free from toxicity because we are not allowing any negative energy to pitch in.

The process of releasing negative energy

Before I describe the process of releasing negative energy, let me describe the alpha brain and beta brain. The alpha brain is the right brain, where the processing and releasing happens in the alpha state. The alpha brain's activity is very slow; it's a relaxed brain. The beta brain has rapid activity; it's the left brain. It is not an emotional brain. The left brain can't relax or be empathetic.

To process negative energy, we need to be in an alpha state or the right brain. If we don't process the negative energy and release it, then we will never be free from the accumulated negative feelings in the subconscious. Without releasing negative energy from the subconscious, we will keep attracting negative situations. During the process, we can actually talk to the subconscious. It is a kind of self-hypnotism. When you are talking to the subconscious yourself, you will talk silently; you will not talk out loud. But if you seek the help of a therapist, the therapist will talk out loud to your subconscious.

During the process of hypnosis, we can visualize or imagine the person or circumstances right in front of us and then start talking to the subconscious. Try to get the answer from the subconscious about what you're feeling and try to find the core feeling behind it by doing this process. Some changes will happen, and we will be able to be free of negative thoughts. We will feel peaceful, and in the future, we will be always mindful about any negative situations that arise. We will then process and release it.

Irrespective of the positive or negative experiences, if we want to grow and expand, we constantly need to rewire our brain. Wherever there is damage, regeneration takes place to heal it. This is the same mechanism when rewiring the brain. The regeneration process is a healing process. New cell growth means new neurons and new synapses in the brain.

If you don't want to work with a therapist, then you become your own therapist. Take the responsibility to treat yourself or transform yourself. In fact, no other person can help you. The rewiring process has to be done within yourself, inside your brain. The neurons will function with guidance or instructions from you. So what are these instructions?

Modifying your thought process means taking control of your own thought process. So how do you control your thoughts? By not getting influenced or affected by the outside environment. Although the outside environment inflicts pain to you, that's actually only because of what you think. If you think about it deeply, the outside environment, which is other people, can't give you pain. They do not act the way you want them to act, and this is causing your pain. But you are the one feeling pain, not them. That means you are giving them power to control your emotions, to play with your emotions, and your body feels pain. If you are always mindful about not reacting to the outside environment, then you will not feel pain.

Concepts of duality

If you understand the concepts of duality, then you believe that in this world, there is duality in every aspect of life. There is pain, which is balanced by the relief of pain. Wherever there is sadness, it is balanced by happiness, Love is balanced by hatred. If you trust this concept of duality, then you will have soul peace. If you want to always be happy, then every time sadness comes, you feel pain, and you peace is disrupted. So believing this concept will empower you to work on rewiring your brain. For example, whenever you feel sad, you start the process of releasing negative energy, and you eventually feel peace.

Some circumstances are difficult to work with for rewiring, especially when we have emotional attachments. I will share my personal story.

It is true that I am writing all the processes of rewiring, but I also agree that is challenging to apply them to real situations. For example, our own kids give us stress sometimes, which create negative energies, but in those situations, it is very hard to go through all six steps of relaxing, accepting, awareness, witnessing, letting go, and releasing negative energies. At that time, it is hard to go into the right brain or alpha brain state or the deep relaxation state, and the tendency to accumulate negative energies in the subconscious increases. The more negative energy accumulates in the subconscious, the more negative circumstances we attract to ourselves.

I have experienced this in my life. I am the youngest of five siblings. Being a female itself was enough reason to be oppressed, and also being the youngest added to the process of oppression. I felt like, throughout my life, I was being suppressed. My voice was never heard by my parents, my siblings, or my distant relatives while I was growing up, and my opinion didn't matter to anyone.

Throughout my life, I just followed my family's commands, which included what my career would be (including what college course I should take), how I should dress up, and how I should talk to others. I couldn't express my frustrations the way I wanted to. Even when I was angry for some reason (most of the time, I had reasons), I could not express it. And finally, the person I would marry was also decided by my parents without my knowledge or consent, and none of my siblings defended me even though most of them had love marriages. Because of these patterns, unconsciously, I accepted that I should follow everyone else's commands. I blindly believed that parents would do everything right for you. I didn't even realize until recently that these negative patterns had been continuing throughout my life.

After marriage, my husband and in-laws oppressed me. I kind of completely cut off any contact with all my med school friends. I blindly followed my husband's path and associations. My husband is also a doctor from a different medical school. My husband's friends became my friends and my main associations. I didn't even realize I was losing my identity until lately when I consciously acted upon reconnecting with my circle of friends. While reconnecting with my friends, whom I could relate to, with whom I had true connections, only then did I realize how much negative energies had been accumulated in my subconscious due to all these negative experiences.

Then I started to read psychology books. I was a physician, but I knew very little about psychology. While reading about the subject of psychology and through life coaching, I started to develop myself, identify myself, and work on myself. Also, I remembered what I learned about brain rewiring from my rehab residency. During rehab residency, I learned through neuropsychology about neuroplasticity or rewiring. The neuroplasticity process is used to rehabilitate various neurologically impaired persons. Neurological impairment can cause physical disability and can also cause brain impairment where neuroplasticity is used in neurorehab for TBI (traumatic brain injury) patients.

I apply these same concepts to myself for transformation. One process I do for my own soul peace daily, and this works for me. Every day, twice a day, in the morning and evening, I light four candles, two yellow candles, and two green candles—the yellow ones in the front and the green ones at the back. I make square shape out of these candles. First, I light the yellow ones, and I pray or wish for whatever I wish for that day. Then I light the green ones and pray for protection of my family, protection from evil spirits. Then I blow off the candles. Afterward, I light a lavender incense stick and pray quietly to remove any black magic done to my family and also to protect my family from evil spirits.

Why does this work? Again, it's the shifting of your thought process—that's the key. Your belief, willpower, strength, determination, and consistency can actually rewire your brain. Rewiring needs strength; only the strong bonds between nerve cells can rebuild the way you want the connection to happen.

Most of the time, I practice mindfulness, and by doing that, I don't allow negative circumstances to happen to me or others to oppress me. Maybe it's because of my experiences, but I tend to overreact or may seem rebellious. I am working on that issue.

In fact, everyone should practice mindfulness. Diverting your attention to something positive when true negative experiences are happening seems therapeutic. Everyone talks about this, but to me, forcing yourself to falsely think positively when reality is negative is painful.

This means you are suppressing negative energy in your subconscious. This is real. Trust me. Simply thinking positively and saying positive affirmations won't help you heal. It is a good thought process, but unless you process negative energies and release them from your subconscious, you will not have soul peace. You also will continue to attract negative situations and accumulate negative energy in your subconscious.

Be aware of your subconscious

Your subconscious is where negative energies accumulate, and you may be unaware of it. So bring to your consciousness the negative energy in your subconscious. This is the first step of the healing process. Consciousness shift is the word. Being aware of your negative energy for which you have feeling and emotions not necessarily mean you have to react. For example, if you are ignored, you feel sad. That's the core feeling. You may also feel anger, but if you express anger, whole process of fighting starts. You end up suppressing that negative energy again, so you can't heal. Instead you accept your emotions and face the circumstances. By accepting yourself the way you are, accepting that it's okay to be sad, that it's okay to be angry, you are starting the process of loving yourself. If you react or express your emotions outside of yourself, that means you are giving others power over your happiness. You are the only one responsible for your happiness. So whenever you go through negative emotions, be mindful of identifying the emotions, accepting them, witnessing them, experiencing them, and releasing them. Try to learn to accept and forget the negative circumstances and forgive the person involved in inflicting the pain to you.

Journaling is another way of rewiring for resilience. How do you become resilient by journaling? When you write a journal, you are actually doing the process of releasing your negative energy. When you start writing down the memories, you are, in fact, reviewing your stories about your life, and by reviewing them, you are identifying yourself and the accumulated energy in your subconscious.

While writing, you clearly identify yourself, your emotions, and your feelings; but you are not reacting. Rather, you are re-experiencing the circumstances and quietly witnessing them and then letting go of your negative energy and releasing it. You are forgiving the person or circumstances that gave you pain. By forgiving, you can heal. While forgiving, you're already starting the process of rewiring your brain.

Also, when you are journaling, you are being honest and truthful. You don't hide anything, and the healing starts when the truth is revealed. You suffer from pain when you try to lie or hide the truth. That's how therapists help you heal; it's because you are honest with the therapist. Therapists don't judge you; that's why you tell the truth, and you heal. Consistently working with a therapist is a practice of rewiring your brain. Eventually, after many sessions with the therapist, you are already transformed, meaning your brain has been rewired and you are healed.

This same concept applies to both journaling and working with a therapist. In both conditions, you are honest. If you think deeply, you will come to know that if you hide something, you suffer from anxiety. You can never heal if you hide the truth. You suffer from guilt, shame, embarrassment, and dishonesty. Once you reveal the truth, you feel relieved, and you start the process of healing. So for healing, start practicing truthfulness. Start releasing the accumulated negative things hidden inside. Start to express it and avoid any new lies. You will heal.

When you hide your emotions and don't express your feelings, what is that called? It is called emotional debt. Why do you hide your emotions? Because you don't have courage to express them, thinking you will be judged. You don't trust yourself. Trust is love. When you don't trust yourself, it means you don't love yourself. You are always influenced by your thoughts, that you are not good enough, so you feel embarrassed to express your emotions. By hiding your emotions, you are letting negative thoughts, toxic energy, and distorted your feelings and emotions accumulate in your subconscious. By being in emotional debt, you are probably temporarily managing your stress to hide but not releasing or not healing. When this toxic energy overflows, then you burst and express these feelings in toxic forms. This is called toxic nostalgia.

What is toxic nostalgia?

Toxic nostalgia refers to the process of expressing in an exaggerated manner some hidden negative emotions are the associated memories are triggered. Some incidents probably remind you of very painful memories and causes you severe emotional pain. You never healed from those incidents, and the emotions related to those painful memories were never expressed, leading to emotional debt. Later on, when certain incidents remind you of those painful memories, these painful emotions reawaken within you, coming to life again. Those feelings can lead you to take action before you are even aware of them.

In toxic nostalgia, your actions are aggressive, impulsive, and resentful. You start to express your emotions before even thinking, and the words you use may hurt others. So rewiring is needed to manage these emotions. Be mindful before you express your emotions. For that, you need mindful practice, which means rewiring your brain.

When some old painful memories are reawakened within you due to a new event, you have to be mindful. Try to watch what is happening within you. Are these your true feelings regarding the present situation, or are you just experiencing these feelings due to present situation reminding you of those painful memories? When you are mindful, you have control over your emotions. You can control the temptation to react. You either don't react or react logically. Through the rewiring process, you have full control over your brain activity. It is possible that by practicing mindfulness and through repeated practice, you are rewiring your brain, and healing will occur. As your brain is rewired in a new healthy network, your expression of emotions become healthy and natural, not irrational.

Healing actually occurs when unexpressed emotions are expressed in a healthy way and you clear the subconscious of them. It's like having a deep-seated wound that is covered with a scar without draining pus or without debridement. The wound will never heal. From outside, it looks like a healed scar, but there is still a chronic debilitating pain that's deep seated. To heal that wound, you have to suffer from the painful process of draining or debridement to clear all toxic parts out of the body. Same principle applies to healing emotional wounds. Once you clean the base of the wound and clear all toxic products and cover with scar, then the scar mark will be there forever, but you won't feel pain.

The same goes when you clear all painful memories or negative energy. The old memories will be there forever because you can't undo what has happened already, but you will not feel pain or negativity anymore because you have cleared the toxic energy. After rewiring your brain, you are healed, and you won't feel the pain from the old memories anymore. Not only that, but you will also learn to clear new negative energy as soon as it emerges. In life, negative energy will keep coming. That's life. We all have to learn to rewire our brain so that we can maintain balance in our life.

The key to happiness is rewiring your brain. All the problems start with our thinking process, and we can change our way of thinking process by rewiring our brain and by practicing mindfulness and meditation.

In life, we have a tendency to blame others for our pain or any negative experiences. For example, if someone sees you in the morning and doesn't greet you, you immediately start to feel neglected and start to think that the person is mean, or you start to think that you have less worth. But in reality, that person probably isn't purposely ignoring you and may just have been preoccupied with their thoughts. They probably may not have noticed you or thought to greet you.

So who is feeling the pain? You. And for such an unnecessary reason, an unreal thing. But you feel pain, and you will carry this pain with you for a long period of time unless you take a moment and be mindful and think, "Wait a minute. What am I thinking? This is not fact." Or even if you feel ignored, you can just let go of the thought, clear the negativity, and move on. You can think like this in every negative situation.

Reevaluating your thought process is rewiring your brain. By blaming others, the brain network is not going to help you. But we always try to change the outside environment—in this case, other people—which, in reality, is not possible. So if you want change or peace of the soul, you need to work on yourself—not by changing the reality, but by changing your thought pattern. That's the rewiring your brain.

The brain can't differentiate between reality and just the thought process. Brain activity releases neurotransmitters and hormones according to our thought process. So this principle applies by doing visualization exercise. We can truly feel happy if we visualize joyful events and do visualization meditation every day. By doing visualization meditation, we can rewire our brain and feel permanent joy in our life.

It takes time and practice, and it is a long-term process to rewire our brain. I can give one example of a visualization meditation exercise, something that you can do every day if you want peace and joy. If you want to feel loved, you can do this visualization meditation.

Sit in a comfortable, calm, and peaceful place either at your home or any of your favorite places (e.g., park, beach). Find a specific time to make sure you will not be distracted for at least ten minutes. (You can start with 10 min every day; as you gain skill, you can increase your time slowly.) You can light a candle, a scented candle, or an incense stick. You also have to set a fixed schedule every day to practice this meditation.

Sit upright with keeping your spine straight. Place your arms on the side or on your lap, whatever feels comfortable to you. Relax all your muscles, especially your shoulders. Take a few deep breaths. At the same time, watch your chest and abdominal movements during inhalation and exhalation. Watch how your chest and belly rise during inhalation and contracts during exhalation.

Now imagine you are sitting on soft green grass with scented bright flowers all around you. You are smiling and sitting with your romantic partner, who is holding your hand and touching your forehead with warmth of love. You feel peace inside. You feel loved. The love of your life is sitting right next to you. You feel supported, protected, respected, empowered, prioritized, and valued. You feel like you will never be lonely, and the kindness of your partner is touching your heart. You feel so light inside. There is no heaviness inside. You feel like all the burdens of the negative energy inside you are being released, and you feel energetic, joyful, relieved, calm, and joyful.

For the next 10 minutes, count every breath you take during inhalation and exhalation. At the end of 10 minutes, you will see you will feel more calm, content, and peaceful. Then before opening your eyes, move your fingers and toes a couple of times. Rub your palm, and touch your eyes with your warm palm. Then slowly open your eyes. You will feel refreshed.

By doing the above exercise every day, your brain will learn that you are truly loved in real life. This is rewiring the brain or neuroplasticity exercise. The brain is rewired with new neural connections.

Taking a new route also helps in rewiring your brain. Every time you learn a new skill, the potential to rewire your brain increases. When you are learning something new, it helps in two ways. First, you are so focused in learning the new skill that you are already in the process of healing. You are not focusing in your negativity, so your brain is not sensing any negativity or painful stimuli. Second, you are exercising this new skill and giving positive stimuli to brain, so the brain will signal and transmit positive energy throughout your body. You will eventually feel peaceful, and your brain will sense only new positive energy. Overall, new neural connections are set up.

When you are involved in activities that satisfy you, it promotes healing through the rewiring process. It's not like you will be completely healed or will not experience negative circumstances anymore, but even when you will face negative situations, if you are skilled in the rewiring process, you will be able to cope with challenges better because of these neuroplasticity exercises. Any new activity that is pleasant to you will improve the neuroplasticity of the brain.

Rewire your brain by forgiving

When someone does something wrong to you, you develop grudges within you. But what happens to your brain when you cling to a grudge?

The parts of your brain that specialize in criticism grow more active. They feed on your thoughts about the grudge. The neurons involved lay down more connections, strengthening this response. So your brain center, which is responsible for giving a response to criticism, becomes strong and powerful (full of energy). This part of the brain becomes very energized and remains active that the next time someone behaves in a way you disapprove of, your brain more readily jumps to criticism and judgment. So you become judgmental. Sometimes, without even thinking or considering the consequences, you inflict pain to others by judging them. All that is understandable. You're not alone in throwing out criticisms, but there's a price to pay for this.

The same parts of your brain that criticize others also criticize yourself. You tend to become more unforgiving about your own mistakes. Self-acceptance recedes. It becomes harder for you to like yourself. Further, this can lead to a cycle of mutual criticism between you and the people who matter to you. It tends to weaken the supportive relationships we all need.

Give yourself the gift of forgiveness, strengthen your resolve to do what is good and important going forward, and then move on. This same gift of forgiveness may be given to others as you recognize the fact that all human beings are vulnerable to errors or even terrible behavior.

Forgiving yourself and others heals your brain. When you forgive people, it lets you let go of your negative energy and helps you release it. And by releasing this energy, you start the whole process of healing by clearing your subconscious.

You forgive people who did you wrong not because they deserve it but for your own peace. If you keep grudges, you are strengthening your brain center of criticism, you start to judge yourself too, and eventually, when you realize that you are making the same mistake that others made, then you start to hate yourself. When you hate yourself, you can't love yourself and can't take care of yourself. Then you suffer from anxiety and guilt, and the cycle goes on and on. Your brain network with this toxic energy will starts to grow strong, and it is very hard to break that connection.

So start forgiving others for your own healing. Forgiveness rewires your brain and strengthens your new neural connection in the forgiveness center, and you will have empathy for others, will hold no grudges, and will have peace.

The more you practice understanding and forgiveness, starting with yourself, the more you strengthen the self-reassuring parts of your brain. These are the same parts that show empathy and compassion to others. They make you more accepting of yourself despite all your flaws and stumbles.

We all have flaws and stumbles. That's okay. It's part of being human.

For a better quality of life, for more self-acceptance, and for a lower risk of cognitive decline, try loosening your grip on grudges. Be gentle with yourself when you slip up in this effort. The steering wheel of your life often requires a little time, patience, and practice before you can turn it reliably. Keep practicing, and one day, you will be able to acquire the skill.

Sometimes, even when you forgive, negative memories and toxic energy will keep coming back to you repeatedly. What do you do then? Try this.

Here's an example: One of your best friends hurts you repeatedly by insulting you. You forgive her/him, but as you are trying to let go of your negativity, you find that you are still not able to clear the negative energy. Then you can destroy all evidence related to memories of her/his. For example, in the past, that person may have given you a birthday card with a very touching note, so you kept that right in front of you on your work desk. But now, every time you look at that card, it reminds you of painful memories not good memories of that person. Then you can just tear off that card.

I have tried that recently. Let's see if it works. I trust it will work.

I think that by doing this, you are actually clearing negative energy both from inside and outside. But don't forget to forgive that person. Don't wish anything bad for them. Continue to send blessings to them by praying to God for them. When you pray for others and for yourself, you feel peace inside, just like the way you feel good if you are passionate about helping others. You feel good when you help others.

Rewiring your brain by being resilient

When you think positive about yourself consistently, you become emotionally resilient by being emotionally intelligent. Rewiring your brain strengthens the brain tissue and neural connections, and when your brain connections are strong, you are emotionally intelligent.

When you experience negative circumstances, change your feelings from negative to positive, and do so repeatedly. Consciously or mindfully practice these, and eventually, you will become resilient by rewiring your brain.

Please look at the picture below:

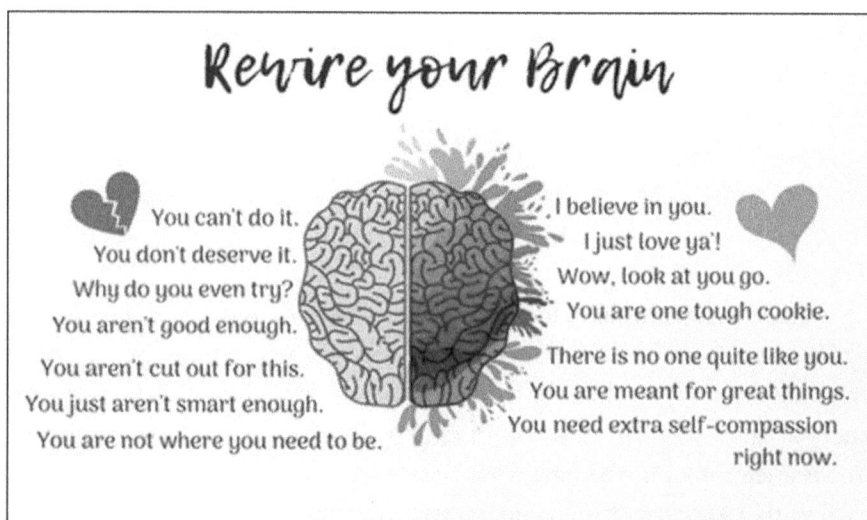

Rewire your Brain

You can't do it.
You don't deserve it.
Why do you even try?
You aren't good enough.
You aren't cut out for this.
You just aren't smart enough.
You are not where you need to be.

I believe in you.
I just love ya'!
Wow, look at you go.
You are one tough cookie.
There is no one quite like you.
You are meant for great things.
You need extra self-compassion right now.

When you doubt your abilities, then repeat to yourself: "I can do it." When you feel that you don't deserve something, tell yourself that you love yourself, that you are the best. Love yourself unconditionally. You don't need to prove yourself to feel worthy of anything. When you feel like you are not good enough, tell yourself that you are one tough cookie. When you feel like you are not smart enough, tell yourself that you are meant for great things. You were born to do great things in life, but others surrounding you might not see those qualities.

Rewiring your brain through art

Brain scans indicate that artists have more gray matter in the area of the brain called the precuneus in the parietal lobe. That region is involved with many skills but is possibly linked to the control of your mind's eye for visual creativity.

Artists usually use their right brain for their creative work. In other words, to do any kind of art, you have to go use the alpha state or the right brain. The left brain or beta brain is responsible for intellectual activities, logical activities. The alpha brain is called the relaxed brain or relaxed state, which is crucial for healing. And the healing process occurs in the alpha brain. Artists heal their trauma through using the right brain in creative work and eventually through visual creativity.

There is an increasing amount of scientific evidence that proves art enhances brain function. It has an impact on brain wave patterns and emotions and the nervous system and can actually raise serotonin levels. Art can change a person's outlook and the way they experience the world.

An artist's perception of the world is different from that of non-artists. An artist has a different vision, a different thought process. The negative energy stored in their subconscious can be released in different ways. If you are a painter, you release through painting in different colors. The different colors may have a certain meaning to you that's different to how viewers perceive them. Painters try to make their life colorful through their artwork. When some life experiences are hard to accept, we balk and fret. We suffer from anxiety, depression, and tension. As tension develops inside, artists try to relieve the stress through art.

When painters paint, they are helping themselves heal in two ways.

First, by focusing on the art (the painting), they are actually meditating, and as they work in that moment, they forget the past and do not worry about the future. Their brain and mind are blended with their artwork. Whatever the type of the art—painting, singing, dancing, writing, acting, etc.—the process is the same.

Second, they are releasing the negative energy from their subconscious. The door of the subconscious opens the moment you start doing the artwork. And just as the negative energy was stored in your subconscious without your knowledge and started inflicting pain, it is released in the same way—without your conscious knowledge through artwork.

Some people keep their pain inside for years and years. They can't express it to anyone because of they are too embarrassed or find it difficulty in expressing it. So instead they express their pain through art.

The process of creating an artwork releases the negative energy from the subconscious, and artists (whether professional artists or hobbyists) rewire their brain by regularly engaging in artistic activities.

Art allows people to enter a flow state or that feeling of being "in the zone," where you lose sense of yourself and time. Making art can help you be more present, and it activates a variety of networks, including the relaxed reflective state, focused attention, and pleasure.

The following are the benefits of art therapy:

1. Reduces stress
2. Improves focus
3. Processes emotions
4. Allows for the imagination of a more hopeful future
5. Improves communication skill

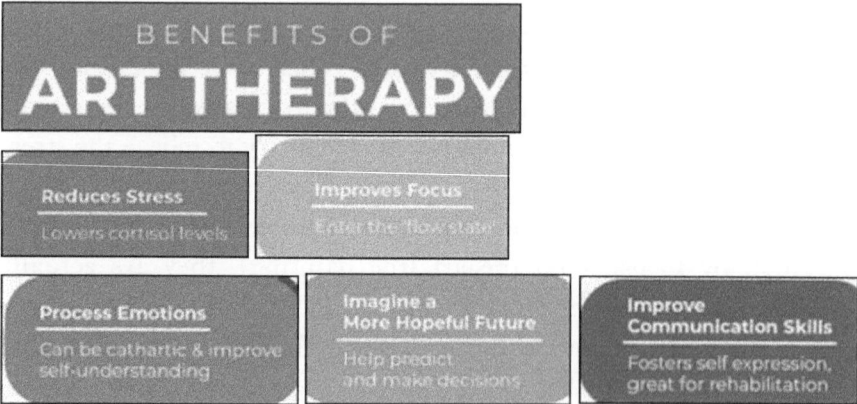

BENEFITS OF
ART THERAPY

Reduces Stress
Lowers cortisol levels

Improves Focus
Enter the 'flow state'

Process Emotions
Can be cathartic & improve self-understanding

Imagine a More Hopeful Future
Help predict and make decisions

Improve Communication Skills
Fosters self expression, great for rehabilitation

Artists have the ability to not only stimulate their own brain's pleasure center but also extend the stimulation to viewers by creating meaningful art. A thought-provoking and complex art piece gives stimulation to viewers, and the viewers start to process that through themselves and go through the same steps—the release of their negative energy—as the painter did when they painted that piece.

The same applies to when you listen to a song. You not only feel joyful because of the melodious tune, but you also try to analyze the lyrics and relate them to your thoughts and emotions. Of course, not all songs give you pleasure. Certain songs can trigger painful memories of bad experiences, but this is still part of the healing process. Remember the six steps. The fifth step is direct experience. So singers are not only relieving stress by singing; they are also helping others heal.

Artists in different categories are rewiring their brains and helping others rewiring theirs. That's why art is listed as part of the rewiring process or the neuroplasticity exercises.

Art is a vast topic. We have many forms of art everywhere. You just have to look for the type of art that suits you. God's creation is full of art. When you go on the top of a mountain, you are at a wide space and can easily see the beauty of creation, and many creative thoughts arise. An artist's brain is wide, like the top of the mountain. When you enjoy nature, there is peace in your soul. The process of feeling peace by viewing nature is created by God. In the same way, artists feel peace through their creative nature.

Art is a kind of visualization meditation. To practice visualization meditation, go into a deep relaxation state, which is the right brain or alpha brain state, and then after taking a few deep breaths, visualize or fantasize the moments of your life that gave you happiness and contentment. Recall events that happened to you years ago, but visualize them in a way that will make as if they are happening now.

When you are doing art, you are practicing the same concept. Whatever your art is—painting, singing, dancing, acting, cooking, home designing, or gardening—they are all expressions of emotions. And by expressing emotions, you are healing, growing, and going into a state of bliss.

Art therapy is also known to improve memory and reasoning in older people, helping in the treatment of dementia and Alzheimer's. In modern science, art therapy is a tool for managing people's mental health problems. In a psychiatric center, patients also undergo art therapy even as their acute psychotic problems are being managed by a psychiatrist and the center's whole team, which includes a psychologist, social worker, rehab therapist (who is responsible for recreational therapy). Art therapy is one type of recreational therapy.

Different forms of art stimulate the emotional brain, which is the limbic system of the brain, in a positive way. It stimulates your happy center in the brain, so you feel joyful and content. And this process acts like positive reinforcement and activates your brain's reward system. The more you do artistic activities, the happier you feel. As a result, you want to do even more art. And you are not only helping yourself heal but also becoming a productive, efficient artist.

Drawing, sculpting, and painting stimulate the hippocampus, expand the number of connections in one's brain, and even help expand one's vocabulary. Doing artistic activities stimulates the process of neuroplasticity, which means new neurons are constantly being generated. Strong, healthy neural connections are being built by constantly doing creative/artistic activities of any kind.

The following are benefits of art therapy:

- Reduced stress
- Better coping skills
- Decreased depression and anxiety
- Improved memory
- Increased resilience
- Better self-esteem
- Improved trauma-coping skills

But if art helps in healing, then why do many artists suffer from depression, anxiety, and other mental illnesses? The notion that depression and other forms of mental illness go hand-in-hand with creativity is so prevalent that it gave rise to the terms "tortured artist" and "mad artist."

Painters such as Vincent van Gogh, who famously cut off his ear and ultimately took his life in 1890, contribute to this idea. So does the writer Sylvia Plath, who died by suicide in 1963. Both artists detailed their mental illness in writing.

Popular artists and their mental illnesses

In 1888, Van Gogh sent a letter to his brother Theo, explaining, "I am unable to describe exactly what is the matter with me. Now and then there are horrible fits of anxiety, apparently without cause, or otherwise a feeling of emptiness and fatigue in the head … At times I have attacks of melancholy and of atrocious remorse."[1]

Plath also wrote about her mental illness, referring to herself as neurotic, depressed, and suicidal in her 1963 semi-autobiographical novel, *The Bell Jar*. In the book, she wrote, "I didn't know why I was going to cry, but I knew that if anybody spoke to me or looked at me too closely the tears would fly out of my eyes and the sobs would fly out of the throat and I'd cry for a week."[2]

Plath and Van Gogh were just two in a very long list of suffering artists. Edvard Munch, Charles Dickens, Virginia Woolf, Pyotr Ilyich Tchaikovsky, and Frida Kahlo are also said to have suffered from depression.

Tortured artists are a group so fabled that researchers have set out to discover if there's a verifiable link between mood disorders and artistic ability, but the results have largely proven inconclusive.

Creativity and mood disorders: Similar symptoms

According to some researchers, studying creativity and mood disorders is complicated by the fact that the creative experience is sometimes confused with mood disturbances.[3] For example, hypomanic and manic symptoms can mirror behaviors that occur during intense creative episodes, including rapidly occurring ideas and the reduced need for food and sleep.

In the hypomanic and manic states, the person exhibits symptoms that are very erratic, irrelevant, unrealistic, or illogical, and these kinds of behavior put that person in a nonfunctional state. A manic or bipolar patient doesn't sleep, doesn't have a regular eating pattern, and has no discipline in life. Serious artists exhibit similar behavior patterns, causing ordinary people to judge these artists as manic patients. It is unclear if an artist and a manic depressive patient have the same through processes.

So is there any true link between mental illness and creativity?

Such behaviors also often occur when a person is in a state of flow, a mental state where people become highly focused and creative. During this time, people also exhibit intense and focused concentration as well as a distorted sense of time. But it is ironic that to heal, you need to go into a flow state. So my point is, if anyone sees you while you are in a deep relaxation state, that person may think that you have a mental illness.

It is hard to predict why the painter Vincent Van Gogh and the writer Sylvia Plath took their lives. It could be that they were trying to express their pain through their art, or perhaps no one around them could understand them. Or maybe they could not completely release the negative energy from their subconscious, so the energy was trapped in their subconscious and caused so much tension inside that it became unbearable for them to the point where they were not able to cope with it or achive balance in life.

Healing is all about balance. Famous artists have so much going on in their brain, and their thought processes are so deep that no one can understand them. Eventually, they become very lonely. In my opinion, if you cannot learn how to enjoy solitude, then you go into a depressed phase.

And artists may seem bipolar and depressed because they have moments when they have too many creative thoughts that they want to work on before they wear off. That's when they look like they are manic. It's because they have tremendous energy at those moments. But artists want to complete their creative work pieces as soon as possible because they fear losing that energy or forgetting their ideas in the next moment.

They have these moments of elated mood, but suddenly they lose energy when after emptying their brain as they work on their creative pieces. They run out of creativity again until the next time they have another new thought. This pattern is seen in a patient who has bipolar depression. It is not always true that all bipolar depressive patients have creative qualities, though some do. So it is debatable that artists are prone to develop bipolar depressive mental illness or that there is a link between creativity and mental illness.

Professional artists have a lot of challenges—satisfying the demand of fans, keeping up their high-demand work, and fulfilling financial needs. Artists have to work consistently and have many sleepless nights. And there is scientific evidence that says that lack of sleep makes any person prone to develop psychosis. Even transient lack of sleep can produce some episodes of psychosis and neurotic behavior.

Those famous artists are gone from life, but existing artists can work on themselves and find out how to use their creativity to rewire their brain to form new networks and build a positive emotionally intelligent brain.

Having good emotional health means we are able to manage our emotions, thoughts, and feelings. We can make better decisions and navigate life's challenges with confidence and resilience. Building your emotional health enables you to feel at peace with yourself.

Being emotionally healthy doesn't mean that life will be smooth sailing for you. Our emotional health is dynamic. There will be ups and downs, but it's okay to have them. To rewire your brain, you have to learn how to rewire your brain in order to be emotionally intelligent or resilient.

Treating depression can be done with art therapy. Through art therapy, the person learns a new way or hope to live by creating new avenues for self-expression. Art therapy provides invaluable benefits for people struggling with even severe depressive episodes.

Depression treatment that way is another way of creation. Through specialized interventions and compassionate support, you create new thoughts, emotions, and behaviors. You create an expanded capacity for joy, love, and confidence. You create a new future in which you can live harmoniously with yourself and with the world around you.

Sometimes depression treatment is also another kind of creation—the creation of art. In other words, rewiring your brain is an art and creation. You have to consciously practice these neuroplasticity exercises; it doesn't happen automatically. So the rewiring process is your own creation.

Depression can be very painful and destructive. As a depressed patient, you will want to destroy your life because you lose energy as you express your feelings or needs. You lose the capacity for joy as you are removed from what used to sustain you. It also often silences you as you lose the ability to give voice to your suffering and communicate your pain in healthy ways. In so many ways, depression is about destruction—destruction of your sense of self, your functionality, and the breadth of your emotions.

For someone with depression, art therapy represents an opportunity to push against that destruction by immersing yourself in the process of creation. Through art therapy, you are able to express the pain or deep-seated feelings that you previously could not express verbally.

So depression treatment is another creation. Artists go into a dual cycle inside their brain during a new creation. Phage of Elevated mood followed by low. When artists have low phage, instead of accepting the low phage, they try to suppress by continuous effort of another new creation so that they don't have to experience the feeling related to low phage of the cycle.

By doing this, they are accumulating more negative energy in the subconscious that is never released even though they think they have released it through art. Some of it is released through art expression but not all. And expression is not the process of releasing negative energy; experience is.

So during low phage, an artist has to experience the feelings occurring instead of expressing or suppressing them in the subconscious. When you have so much negative energy trapped in the subconscious, it may burst in inappropriate way at an inappropriate time.

So an artist has to consciously change the process from suppressing to releasing in order to heal or rewire the brain. The rewiring process is a conscious ongoing process. It's not like you rewire your brain and then completely heal. It is a constant conscious process.

Artists will be able to make an art piece that is lively if they can go into their subconscious and release their negative energy instead of expressing it through art. When you express it through art, it is called portraying your feelings. And there is no life in that art piece. People will look at the art piece and will be able to sense the emotions behind it, but they will simply move on instead of going deep into it. Artists are able to heal by releasing their negative energy, and that art piece may also be able to heal viewers. So processing your feelings is crucial for the healing process through any art form—whether it painting, song, dance or whatever.

For example, when an actor acts just by memorizing the script, then he is just expressing the feelings, not processing them. When an actor enters their subconscious, analyzes the feelings or identifies the feelings, and directly experiences the feelings but does not suppress or express them (without releasing), then real healing doesn't occur. In this case, the actor will not be able to heal through art. For the actor, it is just a habit. The actor is doing art for entertainment, not actually for healing purposes. For this type of actor, such an artistic way is okay. But if an actor literally goes deep into his subconscious and experiences the feelings in a deep relaxed state, he will even forget that he is acting. It will seem like these feelings were from his true experiences, and that's the real art. Any art is like this.

When you sing a song, try to go deep into your subconscious and try to associate certain feelings with the lyrics of the song. Then start singing, and you will actually be releasing your emotions—negative emotions. The singer that sings like this is a successful or a real singer. Singing is not only singing in a melodious tone. You have to bring out emotions and give the audience the message that the song wants to express and release.

The same is true for painters. Artists will have to go deep into their subconscious, identify all the feelings there, accept those feelings and not suppress or reject them, directly experience them, and then release them it into the art piece. Then that art piece will be a "live" one. In most cases, artists probably don't realize the process. They rush into expressing the feelings and finish the art piece without realizing that by repeatedly doing this, they are constantly suppressing negative energy and feeding it into the subconscious, making it full of negative energy. By temporarily expressing feelings, artists think that they are healed because of temporary relief for that moment, but the negative energy will erupt in more toxic ways at another time.

When artists express the feelings and rush into finishing the art piece, they feel elated with the joy of creation after finishing the art piece. But when the negative energy kicks in, they are depleted of energy because they have been drained by working on the subconscious. Afterward, they will then have episodes of depression. That's why artists suffer from manic depressive illness.

So art is a process of healing and rewiring if you process it following all the steps.

Go to the flow state of your brain. Release your feelings, not express them.

Rewire your brain by loving yourself

If you are searching for love externally, that love will not heal you because you are dependent on an external source, not from within. You will never feel that you are worthy of love if you expect someone else to love you the way you want. Negative energy piles up when you do not get love from an external source the way you want. You feel rejected, and you accumulate negative emotions in the subconscious without them ever being released because you don't want to go through the pain of rejection. As you suppress more negative feelings in your subconscious, those feelings may be expressed irrationally in an inappropriate time.

When you look for love externally, you will have no control over negative circumstances that may appear anytime. You cannot change another person, but you can change yourself. You know what you want, who you are, and what your worth is. No one knows these things better than you. You have to love yourself first.

What is love? Love is respect, trust, and connection.

So you respect yourself. This is called self-respect. If you have to set boundaries with others to maintain self-respect, you do that. In fact, that's the first step in the process of self-love.

Then trust yourself. Trust that your need is valid. Trust that you are worthy of love. Trust that you are beautiful, that you are great, that you are lovable. Trust that you are at peace.

Connect to yourself, and know yourself. Do you know yourself? Ask yourself what you really want in life. Unwrap yourself, expose yourself, and be vulnerable. Be honest to yourself. Love means being honest, open, and free. You have to free yourself of any shame, guilt, and selfishness. Remember that loving yourself is not being selfish. Loving yourself means taking care of yourself. Unless you love yourself, no one else will love you.

What chemistry is going on inside you, only you can identify and connect to it. When you love yourself, you are nourishing your soul, and you gain peace. When you have peace of the soul, your brain senses calmness and rewires into a new state of calmness and peace. Your brain is at a relaxed state.

When your brain is in a relaxed state (the alpha state), the external burdens you experience can be handled in a sane way. So even in a situation where you feel that you are not liked by others, you will be able to cope with the stress. You will be able to process it immediately.

So how do you practice this rewiring exercise of loving yourself? By meditation—visualization meditation.

Before you practice meditation, you have to love yourself first. In order to do that, you have to know yourself first. You have to identify yourself. Our brain creates our ego, which is our storyline. It's basically a fictitious creation. It's the basis of who we are. We have a strong belief about our personality or characteristics, and we are connected to that specific belief.

If our ego characteristics make us feel like we are not good enough to be loved, then we are fixed into that thought, and that's when it's hard to love ourselves and others. In turn, the same pattern of life experiences occur to us because we attract negative circumstances due to the accumulated negative emotions in our subconscious.

This fixed thought of our brain needs to be challenged. We need to rethink our personality and character, rewire the pathway to our subconscious, and knock the door of our subconscious to visit it. We need to re-evaluate ourselves, take out the negative energy from our subconscious, and bring it back to the brain as a positive force or energy, giving the idea to the brain that the negative energy was just energy created falsely by imaginary thoughts, which are fictitious creations.

The reality is that you are worthy of being loved. Changing this thought process is the rewiring process. It is not that easy to do, but it is possible. So your new ego storyline is that you are an amazing person. You deserve to be loved, and you are loved. This process of changing your storyline, which is stored or created originally in your head, to a new storyline is the process of rewiring your brain, and this is done by meditation. As you know, meditation is done in the deep relaxation state of the brain or the alpha brain.

After consistent meditation exercises, you will be able to see results. You will be transformed.

If you can contemplate this process or any neuroplasticity exercises, lights of hope and peace will flow through your body, soul, and spirit, and you will be content with happiness because of this unending love. Your brain will have this rich, strong neural bonding that is unbreakable. When this strong network in your brain is formed, then you are healed. The purpose of rewiring is to heal from trauma. The brain can't differentiate between reality and false thought or belief. So when you change your beliefs and reorganize your thoughts, your brain will sense it as reality, and you will feel happy and experience joy.

The fact is, to be happy, you have to work on yourself first. Actually, that's the only way you can be happy—by working on yourself. This means you have to change the way you think; you should love yourself. Changing others is not within your control, but changing yourself is fully under your control. No one can give you pain unless you allow them to.

All distorted thoughts make aberrant neural connections in the brain, which disturb your well-being and your mental health. Love can correct these distorted thoughts and bring these aberrant connections to normal. Healthy neural connections are full of love, light, joy, and contentment. There is no darkness in these new neural connections.

A stroke patient can develop a condition called hemineglect, a condition where a stroke patient is unaware or unresponsive to an object, people, and other stimuli (sometimes, patients even ignore their own left limbs) in the left side of space. This happens after a right-sided parietal stroke. In this situation, patients are not able to see whatever is in their left side. That's when neuroplasticity exercises can help. An example of a stroke patient is given here to prove that neuroplasticity or rewiring is possible: "Wired for Love" is the neurobiological story of how love rewires the brain.

What exactly happens to the brain when we are in love?

When we fall in love with someone, the first thing we notice is how good it feels. It's because the brain releases feel-good neurotransmitters (dopamine), which boost our mood. When we find love, it is like experiencing biological fireworks. Our heart rate is elevated, and our levels of the so-called love hormone (oxytocin) are rising. This makes us feel connected or wired together. Our levels of the hormone and neurotransmitter norepinephrine spike, which makes us lose track of time. Our levels of adrenaline rise, which expands the capillaries in our cheeks and makes us flush.

Meanwhile, our levels of serotonin, a key hormone in regulating appetite and intrusive anxious thoughts, fall down. So when we are in love, we might find ourselves eating irregularly or experiencing a loss of appetite—though it's not exactly a loss of appetite but more of a feeling of needing less food. This is because you are so euphoric and content even without having food. You are fixated on small details and worrying about sending the "perfect text" or saying the "perfect words" and then replaying the text or the phone call over and over again in your head.

Then when we start feeling a deep sense of calm and contentment with our partner, certain brain areas are activated, triggering not just basic emotions but also more complex cognitive functions. This can lead to several positive results, like pain suppression, more compassion, better memory, and greater creativity. Romantic love feels like a superpower that makes the brain thrive.

This is how rewiring happens when you are in love.

While you are in love, mirror neurons, a network of brain cells, are activated. For example, you move or feel something, and you see another person moving or feeling the same thing. When you have a strong connection with someone, the mirror neuron system is boosted. That means the process of neuroplasticity is activated, and it is a rewiring process. So you can rewire your brain when you are in love. The same thing applies when you love yourself, right? When you feel good about yourself, you start to love yourself, the feel-good neurotransmitter (dopamine) is released, and you feel content. You can consciously consistently practice this neuroplasticity exercise.

Rewiring your brain with kindness

Kindness means caring about other people's well-being and taking action to help make other people's lives better and happier. The first step of rewiring your brain is to be kind to yourself first; only then can you help others too. Kindness or an act of kindness makes you feel happy, and you feel empowered and peaceful. When we do something kind for someone, you earn their trust and respect, and you feel better about yourself for being a good person.

Kindness is a reciprocal relationship. It becomes a cycle that strengthens our bond with friends, family, lovers, coworkers, and acquaintances. The more we practice kindness, the easier it becomes. Every thought and action we do fires neurons in our brain. The more these neural pathways are fired, the easier it becomes to activate them. So the more we repeat acts of kindness, the easier it is to do them in the future.

Repeating acts of kindness strengthens the wiring in the brain in a positive way. Doing acts of kindness makes you feel joyful.

How do you practice kindness?

1. See from the other person's perspective

The practice of perspective-taking is a scientifically supported technique that we can use to increase empathy and kindness toward others. The aim of this technique is to imagine ourselves experiencing a situation from another person's perspective.

How would you feel if you were them? What thoughts would you have? How would you act if you were in their shoes? By answering these questions, we can gain a deeper understanding of why people act the way they do.

Perspective-taking helps us step out of our narrow mind and see the world through the lens of another conscious being. And by understanding people better, we learn to interact with them better. We can be nicer to them and even forgive them when they do things we normally wouldn't understand.

And by forgiving, we are rewiring our brain.

2. Practice kindness in small doses

Kindness starts as a thought but ends as an action. Acting kindly toward others is the only real way to let people know we care about them and their happiness. Without action, kindness just lives in our minds but never touches the real world.

Being kind to others doesn't have to be complex or fancy. Sometimes the simplest acts of kindness are seen as the most sincere, such as holding the door, helping with directions, saying "please" and "thank you," or even just smiling.

Kindness is like a muscle. The more we exercise it, the better we become at it, and the more chances of rewiring your brain.

3. Pause when you get angry or frustrated

An important part of being a kind person is knowing how to control our anger and frustration. It's natural for us to occasionally be upset with other people; however, we should try our best to channel these emotions in constructive ways—not lash out, yell, insult, or be aggressive.

One recommended technique to overcome these impulsive emotions is called the stop Meditation. It allows us to take a short pause and reflect on our thoughts and feelings before acting on them.

Often, by creating a pause between our thoughts and actions, we can re-evaluate what we're doing in the moment and change our direction if we find ourselves wanting to do something stupid or destructive.

So when someone pisses you off and you want to yell at them, take a mental step back, breathe a few deep breaths, and then focus on the situation with a clear mind.

4. Try a loving–kindness meditation

Loving–kindness meditation is a popular technique in Buddhism designed to cultivate warm, positive feelings toward all conscious beings.

The meditation begins with focusing on yourself and loving yourself fully and completely. You then extend these good feelings of love toward family, friends, coworkers, acquaintances, and even enemies.

The goal by the end of the meditation is to radiate good vibes toward everyone in the world.

By doing the loving–kindness meditation, you can rewire your brain toward positive feeling and then healing. Any meditation exercise is like physical exercise. In physical exercise, you build or strengthen your skeletal muscles. By doing a meditation exercise, you strengthen your brain network and neural connections. The stronger the neural connection, the more stable your brain function. Any act of kindness not only will make those you are kind to feel better but will also make you happy. Any act of kindness actually releases happy hormones if that act makes you happy; in other words, if you are genuinely doing act of kindness, you will be invigorated and will feel empowered, content, strong, confident, and more peaceful.

Let me describe an interesting effect of brain—the cocktail party effect.

What is the cocktail party effect?

The brain has an amazing capacity to filter out stimuli that seem irrelevant or unimportant. For example, imagine looking at a page covered with black dots and one red dot on it, wherever it means. Where does your attention go? Imagine being in a party. You are in a crowd surrounded by many people and acquaintances, and then, at one point, one of your best friends enters the room. Your all attention will go to your friend. Your brain has the capacity to listen to your friend's every word even in that crowd, where all people are talking. There is also probably loud music going on, but your attention is still toward your friend. This is the cocktail party effect. This is due to the saliency of something. Here, the salient aspect is your friend.

Things that create saliency induce the release of neurotransmitters, like dopamine and norepinephrine, activating your synapses and increasing synaptic plasticity. This regulates memory formation. The stronger the salient experience, the stronger the synaptic plasticity. This is because, at that moment, a number of cells are activated, releasing lots of neurochemicals and changing the synaptic connections. This is the process of rewiring. Some of these connections are strengthened, while some may be weakened. This helps change the synaptic circuit responsible for memory formation, making them long-lasting.

Any act of kindness uses the sane process of saliency and strengthens neural synaptic connections or plasticity, rewiring your brain. What is salient to you releases neurotransmitter dopamine, and the temporal lobe of your brain works on keeping memories and firing neurons. This builds neural synaptic connections, and the rewiring process is activated.

There are several regions of your brain anchored in the anterior insula and dorsal anterior cingulate cortex that work to help you determine what is salient. Rewiring or neuroplasticity means building new neural connections. Which is salient and neuroplasticity can also make a weaker synapse and even remove it.

When synaptic connections are removed, it's called pruning. Why is pruning necessary for healthier brain or well-being?

If you are gardening, you need to prune dead branches to make a stronger, healthier tree and promote its growth. The same theory applies to your brain growth and transformation. So the rewiring process includes neuroplasticity, which requires new growth or strengthens salient signals or connections and weaken or remove unwanted or unnecessary signals. The brain has this amazing skill that filters out unimportant or toxic signals. Through this process, you acquire new desired behavior which is healthy for you and remove those behaviors from your life which was literally giving you poisons.

As your environment changes, so do the neural circuits within your brain. This is the basis for neuroplasticity. Your brain is designed to help you adapt to whatever environment you are in. Stimuli that are important to you in your environment become salient, and this changes the synaptic connections within your brain. An enriched environment, which is the core concept that underpins the neurons, is full of salient stimuli.

I also want to describe the aesthetic triad.

Aesthetic triad

What is it? When you are going through an aesthetic experience, what happens to your brain?

The brain receives information through the sensorimotor system. This is the first step of the aesthetic triad. For example, you see a beautiful object, your visual sensory input is activated, and sends this information of beauty to your brain. And then the brain perceives it as beautiful and makes you happy. Similarly, if you are touched by a kind act of a certain individual, it gives you this joyful information.

The next step of the aesthetic triad is the brain's reward system. What is the brain's reward system? This is a set of neural structures or circuits that activate when you experience happiness or pleasure. When the reward system is activated, you probably will repeat the same behavior that gave you happiness prior to the event that sparked it.

We survive because of the reward system. Typically, behavior that activates the reward system are those related to food, sleep, etc.—things that satisfy the basic needs of life. We feel pleasure when we eat delicious food. It activates the brain's reward system. It's like when you reward a person for doing something great; that person will continue to grow and will be inspired to do similar activities. The pleasure we get out of art, either by being an artist or by observing art (when we think that art is beautiful), offers the same basic response and activates the reward system.

The third step of the aesthetic triad is meaning-making. What's the meaning of everything you experience, and what do you make of it? What is your perception of this aesthetic experience? Perception of art can be different to different people. It depends on your background, the environment you grew up in, how you were raised or brought up, etc.

Art and aesthetics are far more than just beauty. They offer emotional connection to the full range of human experiences. Art that spurts multiple emotions becomes salient, which in turn rewires your neural pathways.

If a piece of art can help you express your multiple emotions, this allows you to heal, and it becomes a unique piece of art. Your brain activity or thought process is unique to you. There is no other single brain that is similar to your brain. The way that information is received by your brain, which is the first circle of the aesthetic triad, is different from anyone else's brain. In the same way, your brain's reward system, which is the second circle of the aesthetic triad, is also different. So is meaning-making, the third circle of the aesthetic triad. Meaning-making is your interpretation of your experiences and what you make out of your experiences.

In rewiring your brain or transforming yourself, let me describe a brain network that needs to be rewired for healing or transformation to occur.

Default mode network

What is the default mode network (DMN)? It is a system of connected brain areas that show increased activity when a person is not focused on what is happening around them, when the person is daydreaming.

It's basically when a person has multiple thoughts wandering around inside their brain. The person is in a state of being either in the past or future and is busy thinking about what happened in the past or worrying about what will happen in the future. The person is not aware of their surroundings right at that moment. In this state, the person goes into a rollercoaster of thoughts and may have a lot of stress hormones or cortisol inside the body.

What parts of the brain are in the DMN?

The areas of the brain included in the DMN include the medial temporal lobe, the medial prefrontal cortex, and the posterior cingulate cortex, as well as the ventral precuneus and parts of the parietal cortex. All these regions have been associated with some aspect of internal thought. For example, the medial temporal lobe is associated with memory. The medial prefrontal cortex has been associated with theory of mind, the ability to recognize others as having thoughts and feelings similar to one's own. The posterior cingulate is thought to involve integrating different kinds of internal thoughts. Mirror neurons have also been posited to interact with the DMN.

The DMN's role is active in rumination.

What is rumination?

Rumination is the tendency to keep thinking, replaying, or obsessing over negative emotional situations or experiences. And by continually thinking about negative experiences, you may end up being depressed and feeling worse about yourself, which may have a really bad impact on your mental well-being. If you don't take care of this rumination process at the early stage, you may end up suffering from major depression.

Connectivity between particular DMN areas of the brain has been linked to higher levels of rumination in depressed individuals, who ruminate about their regrets, failures, shame, and anger.

What is the DMN's role in loneliness?

The DMN is more connected in the brains of lonely people, meaning there is more activity in the DMN areas in the brains of lonely people.

But DMN has a positive effect on creativity, and this may be the reason an artist enjoys solitude. There are two explanations for this: One, a lonely person may find a way to cope with the stress related to the rumination process, which is related to the DMN. Two, the DMN plays a role in creativity.

What is the DMN's role in creativity?

The DMN is also thought to play a role, in combination with other brain networks, in key qualities such as creativity. As a person idles and their mind becomes driven or carried along, the activity of the DMN may help give rise to ideas that other networks then vet and process further. So the DMN is also involved in the rewiring process through this creativity role.

Calming the DMN

Relaxation techniques, mindfulness, meditation, and even deep breathing can quiet the DMN. Meditation is associated with reduced activity in the DMN. Researchers have also found that meditation quiets the DMN and boosts well-being through decreased inflammation and stress.

Time spent in nature can disengage the DMN. Joyful experiences (such as hiking to a mountaintop, watching the moon rise, or swimming in the ocean) can take you out of your mind, dimming DMN activities. Your focus is not on everyday worries but more on the big picture. This diverts your attention from negative emotions to positive experiences, causing positivity to grow inside you. Meditation or time spent in nature or any kind of activities that gives you pleasure will relax your brain and fade DMN activities.

How do we achieve our biggest goals in life? Hard work, learning new skills, and staying focused are definitely important things, but one of the most important things we need is motivation. Losing motivation can stop us in our tracks. It can make us procrastinate, doubt our skills and abilities, and take us off the path to success. In the worst cases, a lack of motivation can destroy our goals and kill our dreams.

But where does motivation come from?

It starts with thoughts and chemicals in the reward system in our brain. It continues to develop in our brains and is further shaped by our behavior. This is why neuroscience, which is the study of the function of the brain, is so important.

When we understand the basics of neuroscience, we can hack the reward system of our brain so that we can stay motivated to achieve our biggest goals.

The neuroscience of motivation

At the most basic level, humans want to avoid pain and experience pleasure. Our pleasure-seeking behavior is based on a mental reward system that's controlled by our brain. This reward system is what keeps us motivated and helps us achieve our biggest goals and dreams.

Neurotransmitters are chemicals in our brains that help shape our thoughts and behaviors. One of the main neurotransmitters in our reward system is the "pleasure" chemical called dopamine. It is produced mainly in the mid-brain and then moves to other areas of the brain, such as the amygdala, which plays a big role in our emotional development. It also moves to the prefrontal cortex, which is responsible for thinking, feeling, planning, and taking action.[1]

When we have a lot of dopamine in our system, we feel happy because of it, and we feel motivated to do the same kind of behavior with the expectation of being rewarded. It is like when we get rewarded or appreciated for doing something great; we are inspired to do more. The same applies to our brain's reward system; it keeps us motivated. When we are motivated, we do the same work or even do better after several repetitions. By doing this, we rewire our brain.

When we are traumatized, a part of our brain area is damaged by toxic energy, and the rewiring process will have to be activated. For example, when there is a cut in an electrical system in any room, you will not be able to turn on the lights in that room unless you repair the network connection or reattach or rewire or reconnect the electrical system completely. This is the same for neuroplasticity in the brain or rewiring.

When you do something pleasurable, your brain releases dopamine to make you feel good mentally and physically. This commonly happens when we eat our favorite food, have sex, have a great conversation with someone, or do something we really enjoy. Each time we feel pleasure from doing something, our brain remember what made us feel good. It actually assigns a reward value for everything we do.

Our brain even releases dopamine before we engage in these activities that make us happy. It's the expectation of the reward rather than the reward itself that has the strongest influence on our emotional reactions and memories of what's pleasurable. For example, just thinking of a moment that makes you happy can stimulate your brain reward system for you to stay motivated and keep you happy. Then you will be happy even though your source of trauma is not removed. By activating your brain's reward system, you are rewiring your brain.

Thinking about starting a project at work that we're really passionate about also activates our reward system. This act of feeling the pleasure generated by our mental reward systems is what creates reward-seeking behavior and is a big part of motivation.

I will describe my own experience here.

I started a project of empowering women and building open and healthy relationships between parents and children in the Asian American community through the Rotary E-Club of Heritage, New York. The Rotary Club is a voluntary organization through which club members help the community in different ways. I was selected as vice president of the Rotary E-Club of Heritage, and I had the opportunity to start this project, for which a grant was approved. This project consisted of lectures, workshops, and therapy sessions; and guest speakers were brought to the workshop sessions to give their lectures to educate community and bring awareness to challenges like women and children abuse. This project finally was awarded Project of the Year. Why am I giving this example? Getting awarded for anything gives you inspiration, strength, and courage; and you stay motivated to continue doing such productive work.

Vanderbilt University researchers discovered that "go-getters" who are more willing to work hard have greater dopamine activity in the striatum and prefrontal cortex, two areas of the brain that influence motivation and reward.[3]

Hacking our brain's reward system

Here are four ways to hack the reward system in your brain to stay motivated:

1. Keep growing

When you do the same things over and over, that dopamine rush tends to get smaller and smaller. A great way to stay motivated is to keep growing by doing bigger and bigger things. Having new ideas and working on your ideas will help you stay motivated because of the continuous flow of dopamine.

Taking bigger responsibilities at work or any organization keeps you motivated. If you're fluent in a foreign language, learn how to have more complex, philosophical conversations. Keep learning new skills that will push you to the edge of your comfort zone.

Taking on greater challenges will help the brain's reward system continue to assign high reward values to the things you do. Start by accomplishing small goals. As you accumulate more and more small wins, work your way up to more challenging goals.

2. Use visualization

A great way to stay motivated is to visualize accomplishing a goal—even though you haven't completed it yet. Visualization actually causes the brain to release dopamine. This makes your see your future rewards more clearly and go after them more deeply, more effectively.

When our brain releases dopamine, and we feel that rush of euphoria. Our hippocampus, which is part of our brain's limbic system, records those pleasurable moments in our long-term memory. The more we visualize success, the more our brain associates this visualized success with pleasurable feelings.

When we imagine a better future, we're motivated to keep pushing forward and overcome obstacles in our path. This is why passionate people keep going, stay motivated, and stay focused to progress further in life, reaching for their goal.

Visualization is a great way to use the power of your imagination to keep you motivated to succeed.

3. Avoid excessive stress

High levels of stress are associated with chronic inflammation, which can cause our motivation to decrease by reducing the dopamine levels in the brain. Researchers at Emory University have theorized that chronic inflammation from stress may cause a chemical reaction in the body that decreases dopamine supplies in the brain.

But low level of stress is sometimes beneficial, just like little anxiety is needed to progress. Low levels of stress can actually help us perform better by making us more alert. That adrenaline rush we get from stress can give us the energy to do our best.

But when stress levels are high, it can be damaging to our body, mind, and motivation. High-stress can lead to burnout. In worse cases, it can cause people to quit projects or quit their jobs because of lack of energy—energy depletion due to stress. It can cause mental problems, such as anxiety or depression (lack of energy). It can lead to health problems, like heart disease, diabetes, high blood pressure, and other illnesses.

So how can we reduce stress? I have described in a previous section that deep-breathing exercises, mediation, a healthy lifestyle by maintaining a balanced diet, and moderate exercise are tools that relieve stress. Through these, we can maintain a continuous flow of dopamine in the brain for us to stay motivated.

4. Reframe challenges

Another great way to hack your brain's reward system is to change how you look at challenges in your life. A common problem is that many people see difficult work as an obstacle or simply something they don't like doing.

Instead, we should take the challenges as opportunities or possibilities that will motivate us to be consistent and move forward. In fact, by taking challenges, we are able to achieve something big, which may fulfill your dream without you even realizing it. This will help us look at difficult things in a positive light and actually look forward to doing them instead of dreading them.

For example, if three employees in your team don't get along with each other and two of them are thinking about quitting, don't look at this as a very stressful, terrible problem. Instead, look at the situation as an opportunity to use your interpersonal skills to gather the angry employees together, let them voice their concerns, and then resolve the problem.

It will help them improve personally and professionally. It will also help you and your company prosper as well. You can also apply this same way of thinking to your personal life. If your friends or family members don't get along, use the disagreement as a growth opportunity that will benefit them and you.

When we can see difficult things as great opportunities, we'll start to look forward to them. When we look forward to doing things, it activates the reward system in our brain, rewards us with more dopamine, and increases the chances that we'll look at future problems as opportunities to grow.

Motivation is a challenging part of personal and professional development. This is why motivational videos and motivational speeches are so popular. A central part of staying motivated, even during the most challenging times, is to understand how our brain works. Science has given us a good understanding of our brain's reward system and the chemicals and pathways that allow it to shape our behavior.

Hack that reward system in your brain by taking on bigger challenges, visualizing success, avoiding excessive stress, and looking at difficult situations as opportunities to help others and help yourself grow.

When we master our brain and stay motivated by activating or hacking the brain's reward system, we'll be better able to master our lives and achieve those big goals. Transformation is possible by activating the brain's reward system—in other words, by rewiring the brain.

Effect of stress in an aging brain

We all know that stress affects older people more than younger people. Why? It's not like younger people faces less stress than older people. The fact is, reactivity is different in younger people than in older people. When I say stress, I mean stress at the cellular level. Whenever our body face stressors, whether they're internal or external, a cascade of inflammatory process is initiated. This inflammatory process initiates the release of chemicals and defend cellular tissue. This short-lived inflammation is vital for proper physiological function and for our body's survival when faced with illness and disease. However, if these inflammatory signals become chronically released, it can lead to a variety of issues, including the death of healthy cells.

As we age, this inflammatory process becomes chronic, and because of these chronic inflammatory signal release, older people are more prone to develop chonic illnesses.

This chronic, low-grade inflammation is a prominent molecular hallmark of aging known as inflammaging, and it's a strong risk factor for diseases that are frequently observed in older individuals.

Higher levels of chronic inflammation contribute to more than half of the deaths worldwide and are associated with a variety of diseases, including autoimmune diseases, cardiovascular disease, gastrointestinal disorders, lung diseases, mental illnesses, metabolic diseases, neurodegenerative diseases, and cancer.

Changes in inflammation as we succumb to diseases and older age are relevant to the entire body, so it comes as no surprise that inflammation levels can impact brain health as well. But just like we do physical exercise to keep ourselves physically healthy, we can do those neuroplasticity exercises mentioned earlier to keep our mental health heathy. Neuroplasticity or rewiring exercises are healthy habits for mental well-being.

But inflammation in the brain is different.

Inflammation and the brain

The brain has a special barrier (i.e., the blood–brain barrier) that separates it from the rest of the body. This means that the immune system can't enter the brain to defend itself and keep it healthy; instead, the brain has its own specialized immune cells not found anywhere else in the body—microglia. Because microglia are unique to the brain, the cascade of inflammatory signaling that leads to neuroinflammation is slightly different than the rest of the body.

Microglia maintain the immune system in the brain; they are responsible for the cellular maintenance and repair that our peripheral immune system would usually take care of. This involves defending against foreign invaders, dealing with internal stressors, and of course, initiating an inflammation response. Just like the rest of the body, as we age, these brain-exclusive immune cells begin to deteriorate and chronically release inflammatory signals (neuroinflammaging).

Just as before, these signals are meant to be transient signals, but they become permanently turned on and then contribute to cognitive decline, impaired motor skills, and deficits with learning and memory. Neuroinflammaging also makes the brain more susceptible to age-related diseases, like Alzheimer's, Parkinson's, and ALS (amyotrophic lateral sclerosis).

So transient inflammation is necessary to defend cells whether in the brain and in the periphery, to protect cellular tissue from permanent injury or damage. But when the inflammation becomes chronic, these inciting signals fire constantly and causes permanent damage or the death of tissues. After the death of tissues, either centrally or peripherally, regeneration is not possible. Neuroplasticity or rewiring is only possible when the injury is partial, meaning when there's only a milder form of inflammation. But when death of brain tissue occurs, then rewiring is not possible.

Takeaway

There are a lot that scientists who still don't understand the phenomena of inflammation, but whether it occurs in the brain or elsewhere in the body, so far, the following seem to be true:

- Small levels of short-lived inflammation are an essential defense mechanism against various cellular stressors.
- Small levels of chronic inflammation *can* be associated with healthy aging, but chronic inflammation also predisposes us to a variety of diseases, such as cardiovascular and neurodegenerative diseases.

Rewiring your brain through yoga

Yoga helps rewire your brain by developing new neurons—neuroplasticity. It brings mental health benefits, such as reduced anxiety and depression. It actually makes your brain work better by sharpening your brain.

1. A sharper brain

When you lift weights, your muscles become stronger and bigger, right? This happens through the increasing number of myofibrils as well as the increasing thickness of every single muscle fiber (hypertrophy and hyperplasticity). You increase your skeletal muscle size and build strong muscles by exercising.

There are different types of skeletal muscle exercises. Isotonic exercises build strong muscles by increasing thickness, while isometric exercises increase the size of muscles. By doing skeletal muscle exercises, you become strong and physically healthy.

Similarly, when you do yoga, your brain cells develop new connections, and changes occur in the brain structure as well as function, resulting in improved cognitive skills, such as learning and memory. Yoga strengthens parts of the brain that play a key role in memory, attention, awareness, thought, and language. Think of it as weightlifting for the brain.

Yoga builds a thicker cerebral cortex (the area of the brain responsible for information processing) and hippocampus (the area of the brain involved in learning and memory). These areas of the brain typically shrink as you age. Yoga practitioners show less shrinkage than those who do not practice yoga. This suggests that yoga may counteract age-related declines in memory and other cognitive skills.

By doing yoga, you can rewire your brain. The rewiring process is actually neuroplasticity exercise. Yoga is a type of neuroplasticity exercise. Nowadays, yoga has many beneficial effects pointed out in medical practice. It reduces stress levels, which in turn reduces blood sugar, blood pressure, and risks of heart attacks, strokes, and other vascular complications.

Yoga and meditation may improve executive functions, improve memory, relieve stress, increase intellectual capacity, and also preserve the brain's cognitive function. So people who practice yoga on regularly has less memory loss or cognitive decline as they age compared to nonpractitioners. Regular yoga practitioners also protect their brain from damage from chronic inflammation (inflammaging).

2. Improved mood

All exercises can boost your mood by lowering levels of stress hormones, increasing the production of feel-good chemicals (endorphins), and bringing more oxygenated blood to your brain. But yoga may have additional benefits. It can affect mood by elevating the levels of a brain chemical called gamma-aminobutyric acid (GABA), which is associated with better mood and decreased anxiety.

How does GABA help improve mood and decrease anxiety? GABA is an inhibitory neurotransmitter. It slows down your brain by blocking specific signals in your brain.

It is known to have a calming effect in your brain and is thought to play a major role in controlling nerve cell hyperactivity associated with anxiety, stress, and fear.

By slowing certain brain functions, GABA is thought to be able to do the following:

- Reduces stress
- Relieves anxiety
- Improves sleep

Rewiring your brain through music

Music plays a great role in rewiring the brain. It provides a total brain workout. Research has shown that listening to music can reduce anxiety, blood pressure, and pain, as well as improve sleep quality, mood, mental alertness, and memory.

Music is one of the most amazing things ever created in the world. There is not a single person who doesn't like to listen to music. In my opinion, if you don't love music and flowers, you are not a human. Music evokes different emotions and nourishes your soul. It gives peace to your soul depending on what type of music you listen to.

Music helps rewire your brain in both ways, whether through listening and playing (musician). It is a well-known fact that musicians are one of the happiest people in the world. Music is art, and just like any art, it rewires your brain. Music rewires the brain. In some places, music and dance are used as therapeutic tools for patients. Dance therapy is used in patients of Parkinson's disease to improve their gait.

And music is also used in demented patients._Music stimulates the amygdala and hippocampus in the brain, which are responsible for memory and emotions. So music therapy is used to improve the memory of demented patients. When music is played to a group of demented patients, some patients remember the lyrics of the whole song, and they even start to sing, even though they can't remember their own names.

Music empowers you, boosts your self-confidence, and makes your life fuller. It improves your social skill. When you perform on stage, you feel good seeing the audience listening to your music.

Music literally changes the brain's neural connections, creates new neurons, and accelerates the neuroplasticity process. Music with meaningful lyrics can help you heal through expression, expressing your feelings. Listening to music is an exercise for the brain, neuroplasticity exercise. Rhythm, tune, and lyrics can change the brain's chemical reaction and strengthens neural connections through healthy bonds, which help stabilizes your mental well-being and boost resilience.

What is resilience? Resilience is the ability to bounce back to normal after going through trauma or stress. When you are emotionally intelligent, you are emotionally resilient, and the process of becoming resilient requires neuroplasticity. In other words, you become resilient by rewiring your brain.

Music therapy is one of few tools in the rewiring process.

The following are the steps to natural healing:

- Respect yourself.
- Face the truth, and tell the truth even if it hurts.
- Identify your feelings.
- Express your feelings to the person who hurt you.
- Be prompt; don't wait for the right opportunity.
- Be simple; long explanations are unnecessary.

- Be willing to accept the situation.
- Let go of your hurt, and forgive.
- Move on.

1. Respect yourself

Respecting yourself is very, very important. Respect means having boundaries, listening to your heart, and paying attention to your desire. Having self-confidence mirrors self-respect. Respect is love, so respecting yourself means loving yourself. Love means prioritization. When you love someone, you prioritize their need. You go out of your way to fulfill their need, any need—emotional need, physical need, financial need, etc. So if you love yourself, you prioritize your needs first before anyone else's. Self-love is crucial for healing and rewiring your brain. Self-love is not selfish; actually, self-care is important when caring for others because if you are not stable mentally, you cannot take care of others or cannot fulfill your responsibilities.

2. Face the truth or tell the truth

Face the truth or admit the truth even if it hurts. Telling the truth is the first part of the healing process. No matter how much it hurts or how much it embarrasses you, once you admit the truth, you will start the healing process. When you are telling the truth, you are actually releasing negative energy. By keeping the bitter truth inside, you are adding more negative energy to your subconscious and increasing your pain even more. Once you reveal the truth—the reason for your pain—you get relief, and you will not suffer from guilty feelings anymore. If you hide one truth, there will be a hundred more lies you will have to face in order to cover up one truth.

3. Identify your feelings

First, you have to identify your feelings. Pain causes certain feelings and emotions. Identifying those feelings are important for healing. Feelings are subjective; they depend on the individual. Someone will feel pain over certain things. They may appear negligible issues to others but are actually not minor issues to specific people.

4. Express your feelings

Express your feelings to the person who hurt you. No one wants to hear about their faults, or they won't want to admit it even if they have hurt you. Most of the time, you don't want to express your feelings to these people because you fear losing your relationship with them, but trust that your true friend who truly loves you will understand your feelings after you explain to them. If the person doesn't want to listen to you or doesn't understand you, then that person is not your true friend. Having that person in your life will only cause you more pain. A person like this is not worth keeping in your life.

Know the reality by expressing your feelings. Express your feelings and then handle the situation. When you express your feelings to the person who hurt you and that person hurts you again even after hearing your feelings, then just move on. Disconnect from that person. Disconnection or detachment is another process of healing. If the presence of a specific individual gives you pain, remove that person from your life, even if that person has been part of your life whole life so far.

Trust me. It may really hurt you initially, but complete healing or peace will follow after disconnecting from that person. As soon as you start to cut away the negative people from your life, initially you will feel lonely, but eventually you will start to enjoy the solitude. Then you will be peaceful. It's because you have rewired your brain. You've changed your brain's chemistry.

Sometimes, no matter how you express your feelings, even if you do so in a respectful way, that person will still continue to hurt you, especially if their ego has been hurt or if the situation puts them in their place. Certain people are used to doing wrong things and getting away without anyone realizing their true natures. As a result, no one can believe that they are capable of hurting people. They do it in such a subtle way that only the person who has been hurt by them realizes how toxic they can be.

Getting relief from painful stimuli from such a person is challenging. It's like dealing with a narcissist. The definition of a narcissist is that they only care about their own reputation; they only love themselves. They hurt people without their knowledge. When you express your feelings to them, they don't want to hear you. That's disrespect. Be aware of this disrespect, and remove yourself from that person if it's possible. If that person stays in your life, they will continuously disrespect you and hurt you.

Expressing your feelings to the person who hurt you is actually a releasing process. You heal only when you release all that toxic energy. If you never express your feelings out of fear of getting hurt even more, you are actually accumulating negative energy, which will explode later in maybe an inappropriate situation or in an inappropriate manner.

5. Be willing to accept the situation

Accept the situation, however it is and wherever it is. Don't be in denial. Being in denial doesn't change the reality, and it is like denying the truth. Hiding truth doesn't help. It is the same concept as telling the truth.

6. Let go of your feelings

Letting go of your feelings is very important for healing. You have to let go of your painful memories and move on. Let go of your feelings, and forgive the person who hurt you for your own healing. Do this not because they deserve forgiveness but because forgiving them will allow you to heal.

Unless you forgive, you will be stuck with your negative feelings forever. Forgiving the person who hurt you will help you release negative energies. Whenever you feel pain from the negative energy stored in your subconscious, draw your focus to your forgiving heart. You will see how peaceful you feel and how easy it is to move on and transform yourself.

Forgiving, letting go, and moving on—these are the steps to rewiring your brain. When you practice forgiving others, your brain starts the rewiring process. Chemical changes will happen to your brain and set new networks as if you have a completely brand-new wiring in your brain. Old neural connections, which used to spark the electric shock and give you pain, will not be there anymore. That's the rewiring process done intentionally by you. For healing, you have to constantly rebuild, repair, and rewire your brain and consistently practice the rewiring process to keep your mental health stable.

As I said earlier, the rewiring process is an ongoing long-term process. It takes a lot of effort to practice consistently and change or transform old habits to new desired habits. That is the rewiring process. You transform your brain's neural connections to new connections. And if you are consistent and persistent, then transformation is possible.

As I described here, for rewiring or transformation, you need to be honest to yourself. That's transparency, one of the steps of transformation or the rewiring process. Be honest to yourself. Be true to yourself. Hiding the truth is not going to help the healing or rewiring process. Honesty may hurt you at the beginning and may put you in an embarrassed situation, but in the end, it will rewire your brain for your own healing. Eventually, you may feel lonely, but you will feel peace.

Rewiring your brain means neuroplasticity, which means transformation or change. *Neuro* refers to the brain and the spinal cord, and *plasticity* refers to change. The neuroplasticity process changes neural connections for better changes to happen in the brain and transform you into a new you. For your peace, you need to consistently make some changes in your habits and practice it constantly to achieve transformation.

The harder part in the transformation process is letting go of your negative thoughts and experiences. If you grew up in an environment where you were suppressed all the time by your family members, including your parents (one reason could be that you are the youngest among your siblings), you might end up in a relationship where you are suppressed by your life partner, who is supposed to be there for you, defend you, and protect you. You may end up facing this negative experience with everyone around you. It's the pattern you attract in your life, even though you don't want to experience these circumstances.

I will explain through my own experiences.

I am the youngest among five siblings, and I am used to just following commands. I never took a moment and thought whether what I was told to do was good for me. I trusted my parents and siblings so much that I blindly followed their advice or commands, whatever they said.

So I got married to the youngest among eleven siblings, and that was also according to my parents' order. I did not even think once whether he was compatible with me. When you're used to following commands, you don't think about what you really want in your life. You don't develop maturity in making serious decisions. You don't develop self-confidence. You simply go with the flow (with whatever others are saying) without thinking where you are flowing into. The direction of flow decides for you, your destination. You have no idea what is on other side, and your destination is decided by others, though you are the one will face the challenges, not those people who made the decision for you.

So it's better that you identify yourself for your transformation. The transformation process is not a quick fix. The rewiring process is a long-term, slow process that needs patience, courage, consistency, and regular exercise. When you follow commands without respecting yourself, that's when problems start in your life. Dealing with challenges becomes a constant struggle because you didn't listen to your heart.

If you are the one who chose your life partner, even though you face some challenges, still it was your decision. You don't suffer from the stress of feeling oppressed. You will still feel empowered because it was your decision and no one was putting pressure on you. But when your life partner is someone chosen by your parents, even though you probably got a gem, you still won't feel satisfied. You will have grudges all the time, and with every challenge you face, you start to become rebellious. You start to feel powerless and weak, disrespected and worthless.

When you identify yourself, you know what you want, and you start to respect yourself. When you love yourself, you will see changes in society. Everyone around you will start to respect you when you have self-respect. Unless you love yourself, no one will love you. Loving yourself is the beginning of your transformation or the rewiring of your brain. Unless you empower yourself, no one will ever listen to you or will give any value to your words. It works magically when you start to speak up for yourself. People will start to give value to your words once they know you will not allow anyone to control your behavior.

Believing in yourself is another tool to rewire your brain. Trust is the key. Unless you trust yourself, you can't have self-confidence, and if you don't have self-confidence, you cannot build strong networks within your brain. Building strong network connections empowers your brain. It's just like when you have strong social connections. You feel secure and powerful. You feel empowered. When you believe in yourself, you can overcome any challenge in the world.

When you believe in yourself, you are setting your brain in a positive direction. You have self-confidence that you can do it. It is completely up to you if you will allow anyone to control you. Don't let anyone control your brain. You are the operator of your brain, which acts like a computer. You keep downloading different apps through which you find solutions to almost everything. But again, it's a matter of practice. You become an expert on operating any software if you practice, and once you become an expert, you can operate any program with closed eyes because it has become your habit. The brain's rewiring process works the same way.

This is how you should handle different life challenges—through constant rewiring. First, you have to identify the problems; only then can you download the appropriate app to create a solution. Create a network that controls other operations. Your brain is a computer, and through networking (neural connections in your brain), send signals to the respective areas of concern. Whenever there is any default connection, it can be repaired by rewiring.

If you don't update the computer programs, some programs may stop working. The brain works in the same way. You have to keep rewiring and updating the whole network for your brain to work properly. This process of updating the system is the rewiring process.

"Neurons that fire together wire together" (Donald Hebbs).

Just because we build old rigid neural connections that are not healthy for our well-being, this does not necessarily mean we have to be trapped in those old neural connections. By practicing new healthy exercises that are better for our well-being, we can create healthy habits that are better for us. We need to repeatedly practice to develop stronger pathways in the brain with the greater number of times the brain cells "fire" to conduct the new activity, desired activity, new habit. Just like the way we build skeletal muscles through exercise, we build strong neural connections by exercising new habits for our well-being. Even just by visualizing repeatedly, we can rewire our brain and build new habits.

The wiring together of brain cells makes the new behavior feel routine and easier over time. It requires about 10,000 repetitions (a minimum of three months of practice) to develop a new neural pathway and master a new pattern of behavior. This timeframe can fluctuate, as each brain is unique.

Wiring the brain toward wellness

The good news is that you really can use your brain differently and in a way that creates better behavior that supports your well-being. That thought is liberating or relieving in that just as we can become frustrated with ourselves for repeating habits or thoughts that are not helpful, we can also free ourselves from those repetitions and practice new ones. How many times have we talked negatively to ourselves for overeating or not exercising? The key is to begin the new behavior, repeat it many times, and associate it with as many positive thoughts, sensory experiences, and visualizations as possible so that it becomes a new pathway of action and purpose in your brain.

These neural pathways are the foundation of our habits, how we act, and how we think and feel. When we focus on gratefulness and positive thoughts, we strengthen the pathways in our brain to feel happy, and the reciprocal is true when we focus on pain and trauma. It is very important, therefore, to be mindful of our thoughts and to practice and strengthen positive thoughts when they arise.

Awe experience

What does being in awe means?
Awe is the feeling of respect and amazement when you are faced with something wonderful and often rather frightening. Awe experiences

are what psychologists call self-transcendent. They shift our attention away from ourselves, make us feel like we are part of something greater than ourselves, change our perception of time, and even make us more generous toward others.

What is transcendence?

Transcendence comes from the Latin prefix *trans-*, meaning "beyond," and the word *scandare*, meaning "to climb." When you achieve transcendence, you have gone beyond ordinary limitations. The word is often used to describe a spiritual or religious state or a condition of moving beyond physical needs and realities.

Transcendence involves mutually influencing mind–body interactions. It balances mind and body interactions and affirms rather than rejects the unity of the mind and body. It alters beliefs about the body. Situating these beliefs within a religious or spiritual framework can modulate one's perception and experience of pain.

What are some examples of transcendent experiences or awe experiences? What is an example of something transcendent?

Some of the ways people experience transcendence include the following:

- Being out in nature
- Engaging in some form of religious or spiritual practice
- Meditating
- Making music or listening to music or even singing
- Having a near-death experience

One of my friends had a near-death experience and told me about it. He had a massive heart attack, and nurses, doctors, and other clinicians ran the resuscitative process to save his life. Eventually, he was lucky enough to survive. He then later on identified that experience as a near-death experience. He said he was hearing everything around him. Being a physician who works in critical care, he was thinking at that time that he was the one used to making round with residents and other physicians about taking care of a critical patient without realizing that this near-death experience actually exists. He knew everything that was going on in his body but was unable to do anything. He was unable to direct his body to move according to his wish. He had no control over anything. It was all up to our Creator, who controls our life. This is a near-death experience and transcendence.

Experiencing awe can reduce stress, quiet our inner critic, quiet our limitless thoughts for that moment, and inspire us to act more altruistically toward people around us. When we do altruistic acts, we become resilient, and we become emotionally intelligent.

Another component of awe experience is encountering vastness. Vastness is greatness, enormous, expansiveness. For example, if you take a moment and imagine the vastness of a natural creation (like the ocean, Grand Canyon, Niagara Falls, heavens, deserts, surface of the moon), you will experience vastness.

Vastness happens when we come across a view (like a spectacular sunset) or concept (like the existence of black holes) that is too incredible to fit into our current worldview, forcing us to expand our understanding of what is possible.

Not only is awe a pleasant feeling akin to wonder, but it also helps us experience a different relationship with the world around us. The sense of our ego becomes smaller, and as our ego diminishes, our needs, hopes, and purpose become more integrated with the people and environment surrounding us. This way, an experience of awe makes us more generous, and we become empathic. We have more trust in God.

"Awe blurs the line between the self and the world around us, links us to the greater forces that surround us in the world and the larger universe. In that way, awe can serve a dual purpose, improving our well-being while bringing us together."

Like many positive emotions, awe can make us feel good. But awe goes beyond that; it also helps us connect with others. Here are some of the main benefits of awe:

1. Awe decreases stress levels.

Awe reduces stress levels in both the short term and the long term. Spending time in nature outdoors or experiencing awe by travelling to wonderful places reduces stresses. In fact, research is being conducted on this. This means that physicians will probably start to prescribing nature therapy to patients who are under tremendous stress. Physicians will literally treat them with nature therapy; nature will be used as a therapeutic mode.

Some may spend moments in nature while visualizing calmness and peace and will experience awe, which will reduce their stress. When you experience awe, you can compare the vastness of the Creator with how minor your problems are. That way, you will feel peace, you start to feel that you are lucky to just be alive in this whole universe.

2. Awe increases generosity and kindness.

By enabling us to feel connected to each other, we form bonds, act generously, and explore new possibilities. Without an awe experience, there is no possibility of transcendence. Awe makes us happier and more satisfied with life. Awe can impact our mood. When we experience the beauty of nature, we experience awe, and this makes us happy.

While awe can make us happy in the short term, it has long-term effects too. Research has found that people experience awe two times per week, on average, and that having awe experiences leads them to have greater well-being and life satisfaction even weeks later.

Awe makes us feel good. By reducing stress, increasing generosity, and improving our life satisfaction, awe really is good for us.

How to experience awe in everyday life

As awe has so many benefits, we should try to experience it more in our everyday lives. Usually, we associate awe with special vacations or occasions—like graduation ceremonies or visits to the Grand Canyon—but we should make a habit of experiencing awe in our daily lives by many ways. That means rewiring the brain. For example, we should try to sit in a calm place, maybe outside in nature or even in your own backyard. We have a tendency to not sit still in one place for long. We have temptation to move. You can rewire your brain to focus on staying still, sit in one place, and just enjoy whatever you are doing. Think of every little thing around you as a source of happiness.

Though you may be tempted to move quickly onto the next thing, such as taking a photo or responding to a notification in your cell phone, try pausing first to soak in the surroundings for a bit longer.

Create space for awe to emerge in the mundane. While you water your plants, tenderly check for new leaves and buds. While eating, consider the time and energy that went into the food in front of you. Slow down and appreciate the patience and effort involved in habitual processes.

Tune in deeply to your awareness of color, texture, scent, and sound. What do you hear? What do you see? While on a walk, stretch or take deep breaths. We should allow ourselves to sink into the senses that connect us to the world and be in awe of what we find.

While many of us are dependent on technology for work or for communicating with others, it's good to intentionally step away from the screen and give yourself the opportunity to connect with yourself. Somewhat counterintuitively, technology can make us feel more isolated and lonelier by pulling us away from the present moment.

We can stay away from technology and try experiencing awe through many things.

Try visiting a park or making a meal, all without taking a photo or sharing it on social media. Spending time in nature lowers stress and improves our physical and mental health by decreasing blood pressure, enhancing focus, and strengthening our immune system. Experiencing awe is actually very important. It makes nature so powerful. What is an awe walk? It's just walking in the nature and experiencing awe. Try taking an awe walk, intentionally seeking to be awed by your surroundings.

Awe journaling is another way of rewiring your brain. You can think back to your most awe-inspiring vacations, events, and moments and take the time to document them. Where were you? Who was there? How did you feel? This simple practice may decrease your sense of time pressure and make you more generous as well as make you broad-minded and happy.

Journaling definitely helps.

Writing about your daily life experiences will rewire your brain in two ways. One, it distracts your focus from your stressful moments to creativity, and you already know creativity takes you to wonderland, fantasy land. Fantasizing is a great way of healing. Another way that journaling helps is the release of your negative energy, which relieves you from stress. Everyday journaling is a rewiring process. Through this neuroplasticity process, your emotional intelligence increases, and you become emotionally resilient.

Parts of the brain

The brain has three parts:

- Brain stem or the critter brain (doesn't like change)
- Limbic brain or the emotional brain
- Cortical brain (responsible for constructive thinking, an executive function)

The brain stem is the survival brain; it's also called the brain 1.

Brain 1 is the brain stem and cerebellum and is also known as the reptilian brain, which is located at the base of your skull. This is the primitive part of the brain that we take for granted. It focuses on vital survival and bodily functions, such as breathing, temperature, and balance. Regarding change, brain 1 sees it as unfamiliar and, therefore, an unnecessary threat to your survival. Because of this threat, brain 1 doesn't like change—any change, even if it is for your well-being.

Brain 1 is unable to differentiate between good and bad, so at any change you want to make, even for your healing, the critter brain goes into resistant mode, as it doesn't like change. For example, if you decide to change any habit that is not helpful to you, the critter brain goes, "Wait a minute. Change? Nope. I am comfortable as it is." In other words, the critter brain is responsible for your comfort zone.

The limbic brain or the emotional brain is also called brain 2.

Wrapped around brain 1 is brain 2, which includes the limbic system, amygdala, and hippocampus. Brain 2 is also referred to as the mammalian brain, and its primary focus is on love, safety, and belonging. It is the control center for your emotions, moods, short-term memory, and fight/flight/freeze response. Regarding change, brain 2 has to see it as nonthreatening to your sense of love or belonging, nonthreatening to your comfort zone, and it can then decide if changes are necessary or not.

The cortical brain is also known as brain 3.

Brain 3 is wrapped around brain 2, is your neocortex, and is referred to as your thinking brain. As the most evolved area of the brain, it is where abstract thinking, problem solving, and creative idea formation take place. Brain 3 enables us to learn language, be successful socially, plan for the future, and be spiritually conscious. Its focus is on actualizing as a person. Regarding change, brain 3 has to be motivated by the idea.

So when any idea of change takes place, the critter brain starts to freak out, and the limbic brain starts to have an emotional reaction, the fight-and-freeze reaction, and then the cortical brain thinks about whether that change is necessary or not.

It is important to know that your critter brain is your subconscious. It holds all of your memories and makes up 90 percent of your brain. At ages 0–6, you are in a theta brain wave state, essentially being hypnotized. You are soaking up the environment you are raised in. How do your caregivers treat you? What are they modeling for you? Do you feel safe and loved?

During this time, you make decisions about yourself and the world that you consider to be the truth. Whether these truths are negative or positive, it doesn't matter. Your critter brain records them, and they are the narratives you rely on to survive from then and into adulthood.

The critter brain is your subconscious, and that's why it is so difficult to change or release negative energy from your subconscious. Rewiring your brain starts from the critter brain. You have to consciously work on your subconscious. The problem is that the critter brain's job is to protect you, and it doesn't differentiate between good and bad, safe and unsafe. Any change for the critter brain is perceived as a threat to our survival; thus, the critter brain will kick into high gear to bring you back to the familiar comfort zone.

So you have to pass through the critter brain's stubbornness and go through the limbic brain, observe what emotional reactions happen to your limbic brain and stay aware of these reactions, and then reach the cortical brain to logically think if changes are worth it or not. When you are consistently able to pass through these three brains and still stay motivated to make changes and practice repeatedly, then real changes occur, and transformation is possible. You are able to rewire your brain.

I have discussed before that by forgiving others who hurt you or letting go of your pain, you can rewire your brain. Forgiving and letting go of someone or something can help! Doing these literally rewires your brain to dissolve negative feelings about a situation, feel happier in the moment, and train your mind to look for joy and satisfaction in every situation.

Without forgiving, you cannot grow. If you are keeping grudges against someone and are not forgiving, it is actually damaging to you. People often keep their pain alive and don't want to move away from it or let go of it because they unknowingly want to show the world how badly they were treated and want to prove their innocence. They have the victim mentality; they want to show the world that they are the victims and that people keep hurting them all the time. But by doing this, they are actually damaging themselves.

The world doesn't care about your past. The world wants to see your present moment, what you have to give to the world today. When you hold on to old pain, self-pity taints your gift to others, and you will seem like a martyr. You forgive people for your own peace, your own growth. The more you forgive people, the more vast knowledge you gain, and the more you will care less about minor pain caused by minor people or events.

You reach a transcendent state by forgiving. Spiritual peace can be attained by forgiving. Granting forgiveness is associated with activations in a brain network involved in the theory of mind, empathy, and the regulation of affect through cognition, which comprises the precuneus, right inferior parietal regions, and dorsolateral prefrontal cortex.

You cannot undo what has been already done in the past. You need to forgive people who hurt you and move on. But forgiving does not necessarily mean you will let the same person hurt you again in a similar manner. You should obviously set boundaries.

Rewiring your brain through catharsis

What is catharsis?

Catharsis is a powerful emotional release that, if successful, is accompanied by cognitive insight and positive change. The catharsis process is a powerful tool of natural therapy. For example, crying out loud is a catharsis process. You express your negative emotions by crying. It is most important to express your emotion rather than suppress it. Understanding how the catharsis process helps you heal will increase your awareness of the healing process and allow you to take advantage of them.

Having a good cry is a cathartic process. Inhibiting tears creates stress. Stress, anxiety, fear, anger, and trauma can cause intense and difficult feelings to build over time. At a certain point, it feels as if there is so much emotion and turmoil that it becomes overwhelming. People may even feel as if they are going to "explode" unless they find a way to release their pent-up emotions.

The meaning of catharsis

The term *catharsis* comes from the Greek *katharsis*, which means "purification" or "cleansing." The term is used in therapy as well as in literature. The hero of a novel may experience an emotional catharsis that leads to some sort of restoration or renewal. The purpose of catharsis is to bring about some form of positive change in the individual's life.

Catharsis involves both a powerful emotional component, in which strong feelings are felt and expressed, and a cognitive component, in which the individual gains new insights.

Men are known not to express their feelings, and by suppressing their feelings, they are more at risk of having stress-related physical illness, such as a heart attack, stroke, etc. Teaching boys that men don't cry is lying to them about the importance of tears. Women today taking masculine roles at workplaces as well as at home, and they are inhibiting their tears. These women think that crying will make them weak, but because of hiding the tears inside, they suffer the same pattern of physical illness as men.

There is a saying that if the eyes don't tear up, other organs inside the body will start to weep. For example, an asthmatic patient suffers less severity of their illness if they cry. Crying is a releasing process of your negative energy. It is a cleansing process. You clear all negative energy by crying or any other catharsis process.

Examples of catharsis

Catharsis can be used during the course of therapy, but it can also occur during other moments as well, in everyday life experiences. Some examples of how catharsis may take place include the following:

- *Talking with a friend.* A discussion with a friend about a problem you are facing may spark a moment of insight in which you are able to see how an event from earlier in your life may be contributing to your current patterns of behavior. This emotional release may help you feel better and able to face your current challenges.
- *Listening to music.* Music can be motivational, but it can also often spark moments of great insight. It can also trigger the negative emotions related to your bad past, and when you listen to music, it allows you to release emotions in a way that often leaves you feeling restored.
- *Creating or viewing art.* I have discussed the process of releasing negative energy earlier through art. A powerful artwork can stir deep emotions. Creating art can also be a form of release.
- *Exercise.* The physical demands of exercise can be a great way to work through strong emotions and release them in a constructive manner.[5]
- *Psychodrama.* This type of therapy involves acting out difficult events from the past. By doing so, people are sometimes able to reassess and let go of the pain from these events.[6]
- *Expressive writing and journaling.* Writing can be an effective mental health tool, whether you are journaling or writing

fiction. Expressive writing, a process that involves writing about traumatic or stressful events, may be helpful for gaining insight and relieving stressful emotions.

Rewiring your brain by lowering emotional debt

Before describing the process of rewiring the brain by lowering emotional debt, let me describe what emotional debt is.

What is emotional debt?

In the case of money, we all understand the concept of debt. If you spend more than you have, at some point, you're going to have to pay it back, with interest.

But what about emotions? The same concept applies.

When you spend more energy than you have by trying to push your emotions away through busyness and distraction, you take on emotional debt.

We notice this in marriage. When we navigate intense situations that gave rise to intense emotions. We try to put away our emotions because of our busy schedule, other work, and life commitments, and we go into emotional debt, which is difficult to pay back.

So instead of feeling these emotions and allowing them to integrate, we got caught up in a cycle of work and distraction. Eventually, the work load slow down. We slow down a bit. That's when we have to face our emotional debt. We finally feel those emotions we have been pushing away.

And that's how it works. We think that we can avoid these challenging emotions by working more, exercising more, watching Netflix more, eating more, or surfing Instagram more, but the relief we get is only temporary. Eventually, we have to pay back this emotional debt. Eventually, we have to feel again because if we don't, life has a way of forcing us to slow down and listen (upping the ante for feeling with things like accidents, illnesses, burnout, etc.).

So how can you pay off your emotional debt?

1. Slow down

The first step in paying off emotional debt is to give yourself permission to interrupt the busyness and slow down. This can be difficult to do because even when we take a break, we often simply replace one form of busyness with another. For instance, we might take a day off work, but then we find ourselves busy doing random house projects or getting lost in mindless doom scrolling.

So give yourself a weekend, a day, or even just a couple of hours to actually slow down and feel. Turn off your devices, and give your mind some time to breathe. Slowing down means really slowing down or even keeping away from doing anything actively. Give your mind a break. If thousands of thoughts arise in your mind, try to divert those thoughts and focus on the moment, thinking of nothing. You can just focus on your breathing. Just think that you are breathing, that you are alive.

2. Let yourself feel

Emotions like anger, shame, fear, and sadness don't usually feel good, which is why we instinctively distract ourselves from feeling them. But something amazing happens when we break this habit. When we turn toward, instead of away, from these feelings, we learn that we can make friends with these uncomfortable states, and that's when these powerful emotions begin to lose their grip over us.

To do this, shift your attention from the time-traveling thoughts in your head to the sensations happening in your body. Locate the predominant sensation of anger, fear, or sadness in your body, and then notice how this direct experience of the emotion always changes. Just as soon as new sensations arise, they begin to fall away. Emotions, like life, are an experience of impermanence—temporary, short-lived. If you take time to experience each emotion without reacting, then you will realize that the pain caused by these negative emotions are all temporary. If you can pass through these emotions every time those emotions arrive, eventually, you can rewire your brain.

Emotional debt is all of the emotions that you have stored in your body that have not been expressed for one reason or another at the time of their genesis. We all carry some kind of emotional debt. We're taught as children that it is important to keep our emotions inside.

Think about it. As children, our parents quiet us when we cry and tell us that we are okay, that we should not cry. While this is a well-intended act on our parents' front, it also stifles the emotions, and we feel suffocated. We are experiencing pain, fear, sadness, hurt, anxiety, etc., but we are taught that it is not okay to express them. We feel them but could only keep them quietly tucked inside. As we get older, we go through many circumstances in life where we hide even more pain.

Emotions are tricky characters. They are both fleeting and leave an incredible imprint on our psyches when not properly experienced, processed, and released. The purpose of rewiring your brain is to transform yourself and your negative energy, which is causing harm or trauma to us and is not beneficial, into a positive form of energy, and through repeated exercise, rewiring is possible. It is just like physical exercise, building strong skeletal muscles.

Milton Keynes UK
Ingram Content Group UK Ltd.
UKHW040753010224
437095UK00001B/50

9 798885 369497